NEW TESTAMENT ESSAYS

ALSO BY C. K. BARRETT
AND PUBLISHED BY S.P.C.K.

The Gospel according to St. John
The Holy Spirit and the Gospel Tradition
Jesus and the Gospel Tradition
The New Testament Background:
    Selected Documents (ed.)

NEW TESTAMENT ESSAYS

C. K. Barrett

LONDON

S·P·C·K

1972

First published in 1972
by S.P.C.K.
Holy Trinity Church
Marylebone Road
London NW1 4DU

Printed in Great Britain by
The Camelot Press Ltd, London and Southampton

SBN 281 02683 1

CONTENTS

ACKNOWLEDGEMENTS

Thanks are due to the following for permission to quote from copyright sources:

T. & T. Clark: *A Critical and Exegetical Commentary on the Gospel According to St John*, by J. H. Bernard

Faber & Faber Ltd: *The Riddle of the New Testament*, by E. Hoskyns and N. Davey

Oxford University Press: *The Epistle to the Romans*, by K. Barth, translated by E. C. Hoskyns

PREFACE

This small volume of essays originated in the request from the Principal of the Queen's College, Birmingham, and his colleagues, that the Stumpff Memorial Lecture ("The Dialectical Theology of St John"), which I delivered at the College in June 1970, should be published. Since the separate publication of a single lecture is not economically viable, the suggestion arose that I might find a few other pieces to make up a volume of New Testament essays. This suggestion I have done my best to carry out.

The first paper, on "The New Testament Doctrine of Church and State", was given at a meeting of the Durham Fellowship of St Alban and St Sergius; it was followed by other papers dealing with historical and theological aspects of the same theme, and I have not attempted to remove some indications that these papers were to follow, for my own is a little lonely without them.

"Mark 10.45: A Ransom for Many" was a contribution to a sheaf of essays presented to Professor G. Delling, of Halle, on his sixty-fifth birthday (10 May 1970); I am happy to renew the congratulations and good wishes of that occasion.

The Stumpff Lecture is joined by another on St John. This was the Ethel M. Wood Lecture, delivered in London University on 19 February 1970. It has already been published by the Athlone Press, to whom I express my gratitude for permission to reprint it here.

The three papers on the Acts of the Apostles I wrote in German to deliver as guest lectures in Münster University in the summer of 1970. I wrote them in the first instance without thought of publication and mainly in order to clear my own mind on a few matters with a view to a larger work on Acts, but I have translated them into English for this volume, partly in the hope that any serious errors in my approach to Acts may be put right by criticism. Parts of the three lectures (which I hope may be read as a whole) have been used in Marburg, Heidelberg, and elsewhere.

"I am not ashamed of the Gospel" was contributed to the first of what is becoming an extended series of international and interconfessional Pauline Colloquia, initiated by the Abbot and held in the Monastery of S. Paolo fuori le Mura in Rome. It was printed in the volume of the proceedings of the Colloquium, *Foi et Salut selon S. Paul* (*Épître aux Romains 1, 16*) (Analecta Biblica, 42; Rome, Biblical Institute Press, 1970), pp. 19–41. Again, I am grateful for permission to republish.

The last paper stands a little apart from the rest in both style and content. It was given at the annual Inaugural Service of the Theological Hall of Queen's College, Melbourne, in April 1969, where I spoke of theology as an academic discipline in the hope of giving a little support to my Australian friends who would like to see in Australian universities a fuller recognition of theology as an academic subject. The address was published in the *Australian Biblical Review*, XVII (October 1969), pp. 9–20, and I must thank the Editor, Professor E. F. Osborn, for permission to reproduce it here.

There is none of these papers, the Stumpff Lecture and its companions, that does not have for me very happy associations, and I gladly take this opportunity of renewing my greetings and gratitude to those who invited me to produce them, and listened to them with more kindness than they deserved.

Durham, November 1971   C. K. BARRETT

1

The New Testament Doctrine of Church and State

There are few subjects in which it is profitable to jump straight into "New Testament teaching" without at least a preliminary glance at the Old Testament; and this is not one of them. There is, however, no direct line of connection between the Testaments, and the relevance of the Old needs careful consideration and assessment.

For the greater part of the Old Testament deals with a people which was at the same time a State and a Church: an organized political community, with political institutions, such as a monarchy and civil and military administration; and a religious community, with holy places, sacrificial rites, and a sacred calendar. No representative Israelite between Saul and Zedekiah would have thought of denying either aspect of the national life, though undoubtedly some would have stressed one, and some the other. Both aspects are represented in the national law, which came more and more to be regarded as expressive of the *raison d'être* of Israel's life. The same Torah that enjoined just weights and measures, and prescribed specific punishments for theft, murder, and adultery, and an elaborate civil code, also described the national religious festivals, distinguished between clean and unclean foods, and required the Israelite to hallow the Sabbath day.

To point this out is not to allege anything unique in Israelite life. All ancient societies were both political and religious, and the distinction between the two adjectives was by no means firmly grasped. Indeed the distinction between them, and at the same time the distinctiveness of Israel among the States of the ancient Near East, became clear only when, to the surprise of most of those concerned, it proved to be possible for the people to continue to exist as a Church when it had ceased to be a State. When the land of Israel was overrun, and the political identity of its people obliterated, they continued to exist in relation to their God, and to the religious practices he required of them; these practices preserved their unity and social consciousness, and moreover fostered the hope of renewed political independence. From time to time after the Exile the old interlocking unity of politics and religion, of secular and sacred (though this is not too happy a distinction), was resumed, notably under the Hasmonaean dynasty, when for a time the offices of high priest and national ruler were actually combined in one person, as when, for example, Simon Maccabaeus is officially described as "Great High Priest, General, and Governor of the Jews" (ἀρχιερεὺς μέγας καὶ στρατηγὸς καὶ ἡγούμενος Ἰουδαίων, 1 Macc. 13.42). Such periods, however, were brief, and on the whole illusory. Any great power that took the matter seriously could at any time destroy Jewish political independence; and it is the more striking that none of them ever succeeded in destroying Jewish religious independence.

Thus, although in much of the Old Testament State and Church are identified, and the Church's relation to the State becomes a matter of its responsibility to itself—the duty of self-criticism which the prophets exercised on its behalf—in the New Testament period the State meant not "us" but "them", a new situation, which may be conveniently and briefly illustrated by the history of the word *malkut* (*kingdom*). In, for example, 1 Kings 2.12 this is used of the royal authority of the Davidic dynasty:

> And Solomon sat on the throne of David his father, and his kingdom was established greatly (*wattikkon malkuto me'od*).

Behind Solomon's reign lay the sovereignty of God himself, as is plainly brought out in the complicated narratives of the origin of the monarchy, and is expressed in, for example, Psalm 103.19, where the parallels of language with 1 Kings 2.12 are striking and important:

> The Lord has established his throne in the heavens, and his kingdom rules over all (*umalkuto bakkol mašalah*).

In rabbinic usage, however, except where otherwise specified, *malkut* means the foreign, heathen (and usually wicked) government; for example, Aboth 3.5:

> He that takes upon himself the yoke of the Law, from him shall be taken away the yoke of the kingdom (*malkut*) and the yoke of

worldly care; but he that throws off the yoke of the Law, upon him shall be laid the yoke of the kingdom (*malkut̲*) and the yoke of worldly care.

To this account of a significant change in usage should be added one more point. Hope of a restored kingdom remained. At the close of Daniel 7 the promise is made (verse 27) that the kingdom (*malkutah̲*) and the authority and the greatness of the kingdom (*malk̲ᵉwat̲*) under the whole heaven shall be given to the people of the saints of the Most High. It is clear, however, that to the author of Daniel this did not mean the sort of power that we have already seen to have been exercised by Simon the Maccabee. It was not in the ordinary sense political, for it was bound up with, and lay on the further side of, the resurrection of the dead (12.2).

We have now begun to look at the Judaism of the New Testament period, and it is important to note two points.

1. Judaism was not itself exercising the rights and privileges of a State. This statement needs some qualification. The Herod family played an important part in Jewish political affairs, and though not Jewish but Idumaean by race some at least of the Herods did their best to assume a Jewish role, and were on occasion accepted in it. Thus Herod Agrippa, when reading publicly at Tabernacles, came to Deuteronomy 17.15: "Thou mayest not put a foreigner over thee who is not thy brother." His eyes flowed with tears; but they called to him, "Our brother art thou! Our brother art thou! Our brother art thou!" (Sotah 7.8). As long as the Herod dynasty lasted there was a sort of Jewish State, but it was limited in authority by Roman suzerainty, limited and variable in extent, and limited also in its Jewishness.

Further, even in areas under direct Roman rule, such as Judea under the procurators—Pontius Pilate, for example—Jewish administrative and judicial bodies retained a certain amount of power. I shall not attempt here to discuss the very difficult and energetically disputed question whether the Sanhedrin had or had not authority to carry out capital sentences. That it had *some* power is not to be questioned.

With these not unimportant qualifications it may be accepted that there was in the New Testament period no sovereign Jewish State. Jews felt themselves to be an opposition, and normally an oppressed and persecuted opposition, whose leaders stood a good chance of becoming martyrs. This position has recently been described by W. H. C. Frend, in *Martyrdom and Persecution in the Early Church* (1965), pp. 31–78.

2. One effect of this situation was to throw the notion of sovereignty into the realm of apocalyptic. To say this is not to say anything very precise. To speak of anything like "apocalyptic orthodoxy" would be to be guilty of a contradiction. To some the future life was purely supernatural and otherworldly; to others it meant the establishment of an earthly State on the lines of David's, or of the Maccabees', only better and more permanent. Between these extremes almost every conceivable kind of variation was to be found. What is to be noted, however, is that apocalyptic, in all its varying forms, does have to do with God's sovereignty (*malkuṯ*, βασιλεία). All Israel could join in the prayer (the Kaddish): May he set up his kingdom (*yamliḵ malkuṯeh*) during your life and during your days, and during the life of all the house of Israel, even speedily and at a near time.

Primitive Christianity emerged within a Judaism that knew the "State" as a foreign, oppressive, and sometimes persecuting body, and looked passionately forward to the time when God would establish his own rule. To some, this time lay on the edge of history; it could be hoped for and prayed for, but not otherwise affected by human agency. To others, the time lay within history, and its coming lay (under God) within the power of their own right hand, and at the sword's point. The question of Acts 1.6 is thus one that no doubt sprang to the lips of many Christians: "Lord, is this the time when you mean to restore the kingdom to Israel?" According to the author of Acts, this was a proper question to ask, in the sense that it was one to which a precise answer might have been given, had it been God's intention to reveal it; it was, however, God's will to define the future in terms of the religious privileges and duties of his people, rather than the political destiny of native Jews: "It is not for you to know times or seasons which the Father has fixed by his own authority; but you shall receive power when the Holy Spirit comes upon you, and you shall be my witnesses" (Acts 1.6ff).

To the pattern thus set Acts adheres. The Church is a religious community, which has no quarrel with either Jewish or Roman authorities, but does bear witness, in its life and preaching, to the reign of God. The latter, positive point it is scarcely necessary to illustrate in this context, though it may be worth while to note the recurrence, not frequently but at important places, of the phrase "kingdom of God". Jesus, after the resurrection, speaks to the apostles about the kingdom of God (1.3). Philip evangelized about the kingdom of God (8.12). In Ephesus Paul persuaded concerning the kingdom of God (19.8), and recalled the fact in speaking to the Ephesian elders (20.25). Acts takes leave of the apostle with the message of the kingdom on his lips (28.31).

We need not stop to inquire how Luke understood the gospel of the kingdom. He is quite sure that only mischievous Jews could interpret it to mean that Christians were proclaiming a rival to Caesar, as when, at Thessalonica, failing to get hold of Paul, they dragged Jason and certain brothers before the politarchs, alleging that they were acting contrary to the decrees of Caesar, and saying that there was another king, Jesus (17.5ff).

In fact, as has very often been observed, the Roman authorities are represented in Acts as almost invariably favourable to Christians. Paul himself is a Roman citizen, and does not hesitate to make use of the advantages which his citizenship conferred on him. In Cyprus the Proconsul, Sergius Paulus, not unnaturally impressed by the misfortunes of his magus or false prophet, Bar-Jesus, actually becomes a believer (13.12—it is hard to make Luke's ἐπίστευσεν mean less than this, though we have no confirmatory evidence for his conversion, and hear no more of Sergius Paulus). At Philippi the magistrates (στρατηγοί) behave at first in a high-handed manner, but become very civil when they learn the truth (16.38f). The Areopagus court (whom, rightly or wrongly, Luke appears to have in mind at 17.19) hears Paul with some courtesy, though the resurrection is more than they can stomach (17.32). Gallio, notoriously, "cared for none of those things" (18.17), but the effect of his non-intervention is to give Christians a free hand, with the implication that their activities are recognized as not being seditious. In Ephesus Demetrius and his friends (19.24) are obviously actuated by money-grubbing motives, and the town clerk declares, one hopes with some exaggeration, that these men—Paul and his colleagues—have not spoken ill of the goddess. From the time of his arrest in Jerusalem Paul receives unfailing consideration from Roman authorities, civil and military.

Such trouble as arises is always caused by Jews. They do their best to incite the Romans against the Christians, and take such action as they can themselves. Stephen they stone, and after his martyrdom a general persecution scatters the bulk of the Church (8.1, 4; 11.19). The main persecutor is Saul the Jew, who later is himself attacked by Jews as never by Romans. It is to Jews (a significant point) that Peter says, "Judge yourselves whether it is right to listen to God, or to you" (4.19), and, "One must obey God rather than men" (5.29). One would have supposed that the word of God would have been heard, if anywhere, on the lips of Jewish authorities; in fact, they contradict it, so that listeners must choose between the one and the other.

Luke's attitude seems quite clear. The Jews have forfeited their claim to be either politically or religiously the people of God; this they have done in their rejection of Jesus. Individual Jews, indeed, may, and do, repent and believe, but in doing so they become members of a new people. There is no quarrel with the Romans, who found Jesus innocent (see especially Acts 3.13), and reach no different conclusion with regard to his disciples. Their protection may be sought and enjoyed; they are—for the present at least —God's servants. The whole may be summed up in words from the Lucan version of the Marcan apocalypse: "Jerusalem shall be trampled by the Gentiles, until the times of the Gentiles are completed (ἄχρι οὗ πληρωθῶσιν καιροὶ ἐθνῶν)" (Luke 21.24).

This quotation, of words attributed to Jesus, may, however, be taken as setting for us the main problem that must occupy us in this paper. Is it possible to determine the attitude to the State of Jesus himself? How did the early Church build upon this? How far was it retained, how far modified, in the light of the new circumstances into which the Church emerged, as time moved on, and its geographical spread increased?

First, we shall turn to the Gospels; and it will, I think, be right to begin with the most explicit passage of all, Mark 12.13–17 (and parallels); if we can establish firm ground here, it will help us with the interpretation of other passages. Not that all is clear in regard to Mark 12.13–17. Some hold that it supplies the key for the New Testament doctrine of the State; others that it contributes nothing of substance to the general question.

We begin with the setting. Mark introduces the Passion Narrative with a series of questions, of which the overall purpose is no doubt to make the Passion Narrative itself historically intelligible, and at the same time to show the practical and theological interests that lay behind it and gave meaning to it. After the triumphal entry follow the cursing of the fig tree and the cleansing of the Temple; then the question about authority; the parable of the wicked husbandmen; the question about tribute money; the question about the resurrection; the question about the first commandment; and finally Jesus' question about the interpretation of Psalm 110, the woes on the scribes and Pharisees, and the commendation of the poor widow. Within the series of questions the parable of the wicked husbandmen stands out, and it probably owes its place to Mark's own editing; this observation is reinforced by the ἐν παραβολαῖς (plural) of 12.1—this parable was perhaps taken out of a group of several. If we ask why Mark caused it to stand here, it is not difficult to find an answer.

(*a*) It provides a more explicit answer to the question of 11.27–33 than that paragraph itself gives. What was the authority of Jesus? This was a question to which Jesus himself did not see fit to give an explicit reply. The parable, however, whether in its original form or not, gives an answer which Mark's readers will not have been slow to grasp: Jesus was the Son of God.

(*b*) It points forwards, however, as well as back. The mission of the son of the owner of the vineyard was to collect the fruit—the tax, we may say—which the husbandmen owed to the owner. They must (so the parable is to be interpreted) render to God what belongs to him. From this, Mark proceeds immediately to the question about tribute money, the climax of which is precisely the same: Render to God that which belongs to him.

Mark then is using the paragraph 12.13–17 (and in this he may well be quite true to its original intention) primarily in order to bring out the fact that in Jesus God makes his claim upon his people. They must render to him what is his due. The introduction of the question is difficult, in that it is ascribed to Pharisees and Herodians, and we do not know who the Herodians (compare 3.6) were. That they in some sense espoused the cause of the Herods is clear enough, but we have no evidence from which we can conclude precisely what their relation to the Herods was. According to Mark their intention was to trap Jesus, and verse 14 must therefore be taken to be an attempt at subtle flattery. But the fact that, in the parallels, the honest questioner described in 12.28 becomes a tempter, suggests that it is at least possible that here too the original intention of the questioners was sincere. Why not? The question was debated in Judaism. It is of course also true that any public figure who publicly commits himself on a public issue is asking for trouble; this is universal experience.

Jesus does not look ($\beta\lambda\acute{\epsilon}\pi\epsilon\iota\nu$) upon the face of men. This is usually explained in terms of the familiar biblical expression which means "to show favouritism"; and the usual explanation may be right. Mark's word, however, is not the common expression ($\pi\rho\acute{o}\sigma\omega\pi\omicron\nu$ $\lambda\alpha\mu\beta\acute{\alpha}\nu\epsilon\iota\nu$, *nasa' panim*), which Luke has substituted, and it is I think worth while at least to mention a suggestion made a long time ago by H. M. J. Loewe[1] who pointed out that the $\kappa\hat{\eta}\nu\sigma\omicron s$, or poll-tax, was hated by the Jews for several reasons:

(a) No one likes paying any taxes.

(b) This tax was a mark of Roman authority and conquest.

(c) Jews objected on principle to the counting of heads.

(d) But they also objected, or some of them did, to the use of coins (such as the Roman denarius) which bore human likenesses. To use, even to look at, such coins was idolatry.

It is thus possible that the approach to Jesus is: We know you are a good Jew, and will not incur even the minor idolatry of looking at a human face on a coin. Certainly it appears that neither Jesus nor his questioners have a denarius on hand; one must be sent for. When it appears, Jesus actually calls attention to the image and lettering it bears—possibly with the implied rebuke that an exaggerated avoidance of idolatry has caused his hearers to fail to take in the terms of the question they are dealing with. Men write their names on their own property; there is, therefore, a presumption that the coin belongs to Caesar and may fairly be paid to him. How much further the point should be taken is questionable. The denarius certainly represented services rendered by Caesar to Judea, as to other parts of the Empire, in particular the safety and good order that made trade—the use of coinage for buying and selling—possible. So far as Caesar rendered services he might reasonably expect to be paid. But there is nothing to suggest that these thoughts were evoked by the incident. Jesus immediately adds that what belongs to God must be rendered to him.

There is no need to underline the interpretation with the sugges-

[1] *Render unto Caesar* (1940).

tion that since (as the coin bears Caesar's image) man bears God's image, man must render himself wholly to God. It is nearer the truth to say that God has done more for man than Caesar has, and therefore has a greater claim upon him. This connects with what has already been said about 12.1–12, and indeed with the whole of chapters 11, 12, and 13 (with the possible exception of the question about the resurrection). The triumphal entry, though men may enjoy it as a mere spectacle, is truly the coming of the Messiah to claim his city and people. The cursing of the fig tree and the cleansing of the Temple represent God's judgement upon a people more concerned to put up a show of religion than to bear its fruits. The Temple which, as God's house, ought to be a house of prayer, has been withheld from him and turned into a den of thieves. Jesus has, but will not define, the authority to make the claim he utters —he is indeed God's Son, making God's last demand. What God demands can be put in plain speech: it is that men should love him with all their heart, soul, mind, and strength, and their neighbours as themselves; and, in equally plain terms, Jesus is the Messiah, David's son and David's Lord. The scribes and the poor widow are negative and positive examples respectively of what it means to give God his due. Chapter 13 describes the necessarily ensuing judgement upon recalcitrant Israel, and even the Sadducees' pettifogging question about the resurrection is brought round to the point, because it leads to the proposition that Abraham, Isaac, and Jacob are alive because they live to God.

What this means might almost—but not quite—be described as a by-passing of the question about Caesar. True, he has a claim— meet it; but the most important claim is God's. Yet it remains important that the two propositions are linked by the word *and*, which is in a sense the most significant word in Jesus' reply. What some of his contemporaries regarded as alternatives, he joined together.

This does not mean that Jesus found positive value in the Roman State; it does mean that he did not find it necessary to oppose it on principle. It is true that he was crucified on the alleged ground that he had done so (Luke 23.2). No other charge could have led to this punishment. It was inflicted by Rome for a crime against Rome, and the crime was succinctly expressed in the *titulus*, Jesus of Nazareth, the king of the Jews. It was, like the Jewish charge of blasphemy, a false accusation; but, again like the

Jewish charge, it had a measure of colour in it. There had been a show of armed resistance on the part of Jesus' followers, and he had had a good deal to say about a kingdom, and may well have found it difficult to give a straight No to the straight question, Are you a king? His teaching, too, had shown impatience even with Jewish law, and it is on law that States rest. If you can persuade men to be wholly pure, loving, and honest, you can doubtless dispense with laws concerning adultery, murder, and oath-taking; but until this happy state has been reached, society, if it is to exist at all, needs the support of specific commandments backed by specific sanctions. To say this is not to criticize the Sermon on the Mount; it is to criticize society, or, more properly, the human nature which is the raw stuff of society.

This absolute critique—a more radical attitude than the Zealotry that some have detected in Jesus behind the veil cast by the Gospels—runs through the teaching of Jesus. Even the explicit Deuteronomic legislation with regard to divorce is discounted as having been granted "with reference to the hardness of your hearts" (Mark 10.5). Jesus, unlike Moses, prefers to dig into the original intention given in and with the creation of a bisexual humanity. Yet even so he is not without a sense of the practical realism of a political situation. This may be seen in Luke 13.1–5, where he refuses to pass quick religious judgements on political events—the Galileans whose blood mingled with their sacrifices are not to be written off as extraordinary sinners. They were ordinary sinners, and their fate is a warning to all.

Most significant here, perhaps, is the conversation between Jesus and Pilate as this is developed in John. When Pilate asks, "Do you not know that I have authority to release you, and authority to crucify you?" (19.10), Jesus replies (19.11), "You would have no authority against me at all unless it were given you from above (ἄνωθεν)". There may be in this last word a hint at the fact that Pilate is at best a subordinate ruler, but undoubtedly its primary meaning is, from God. As the appointed ruler of the State Pilate does bear (even if in the end he misuses) authority conferred on him by God himself. It would be rash to treat this as an historical remark rightly ascribed to Jesus himself; and even taken as it stands it does not go far towards establishing a positive doctrine of the State. We may recall from the same Gospel (11.51) the belief that the high priest in office might receive the gift of prophecy and so give utterance to truths of which he was not himself aware. Pilate, though on the whole very favourably regarded by John, is not capable of entering into serious exchanges about the truth, and does not even receive an answer to his own question. He has authority to exercise the office which has been given him in the present world order; but in Jesus he is confronted with one who represents an order not of this world (18.36), and the one authority serves as no more than a pale shadow of the other. I shall return to this theme later.

On the whole, in the Gospels the State is treated not in general terms but concretely with reference to its representatives as they appear from time to time. They are part of the given structure of life, just as the seasons of the year and the consequent necessities of the agricultural calendar. As I have pointed out, this somewhat negligent treatment is itself significant; Jesus did not lead a campaign against the State. He proclaimed the coming of the kingdom of God, imminent in the future, and immanent too in his own actions. Beside this kingdom, human institutions, necessary though they might be in his age, become insignificant. Even the law of Moses would not survive the passing away of the present age (Matt. 5.18), and it would consequently be surprising if the Twelve Tables should turn up in the age to come. The whole question is set in the context of the eschatological teaching of the Gospels, and Caesar's claims are but little in comparison with God's.

From this observation we can proceed to examine the teaching of Paul. For him too the whole structure of human life as known and experienced in this world is a temporary arrangement, and it must be regarded—or disregarded—as such. Though it does not deal specifically with the State, 1 Corinthians 7 forms a suitable starting-point:

> This is what I am saying, brothers: the time is short; henceforth let those who have wives be as though they had none, and those who weep as though they did not weep, and those who rejoice as though they did not rejoice, and those who buy as though they did not possess, and those who use the world as though they had no full use of it; for the outward show (σχῆμα) of this world is passing away (7.29ff).

This is a very important passage, and one that calls for careful exegesis. Paul's *as if not* (ὡς μή) stands at the heart of the practical application of his theological convictions. The whole of this chapter is turned into nonsense if, for example, the injunction to husbands is taken to mean that they should live as celibates; Paul has already said explicitly that this is not how he understands marriage. What he means is that a married man, recognizing the transiency of the marriage relationship, should live with the same single-minded devotion to the things of the Lord that an unmarried man may be expected to show more easily. Similarly, he requires not that men should not buy and sell, but that they should, in their buying and selling, recognize the transiency of commercial values, and be absorbed in obedience to God, not in trade. This reasoning may be applied to the State in more general terms. The State belongs to a structure (σχῆμα) that is passing away. This does not mean that it is of the devil, only that it is of the world—this world. Christian men may therefore participate in its activities (though few of Paul's readers will have had much more to do than pay their taxes), but they must not cling to it as if it had a permanency that it does not possess. You may live as a Christian *within* marriage, but you must not as a Christian live *for* marriage; you may live as a Christian *within* the State, recognizing your obligations to it, but you must not as a Christian live *for* the State, treating it as a valid and complete end in itself.

In this study of 1 Corinthians 7 I have brought in the State by analogy. That this introduction of the State into the general eschatological picture is legitimate is demonstrated by other passages which are more explicit. Here I would include 2 Thessalonians 2.6–7, though the interpretation of these verses is not undisputed. They occur in one of the most difficult of the Pauline apocalypses. The end is near; yet not perhaps quite as near as some in Thessalonica, who had seen fit to give up the tedious business of working for a living, supposed. Before the end, the Man of sin must appear: there is no sign of him yet (apart from the unbelief engendered in those who do not accept the gospel), and the Thessalonians should know quite well why this is so. There is at present a restraining force (τὸ κατέχον) which holds him back. In the next verse this neuter becomes the masculine (ὁ κατέχων), the restraining person, who operates now, until he is taken out of the way (ἕως ἐκ μέσου γένηται). What is the restraint that holds back the personal manifestation of wickedness and the consequent dissolution of human society? Various answers to this question have been proposed, but none of them is so satisfactory as the view that the restraining force (τὸ κατέχον) is the Empire, personalized (as ὁ κατέχων) in its chief representative, the Emperor. If this is accepted, two conclusions follow:

(*a*) the Empire has a positive role in God's purpose;
(*b*) this role is a temporary role—it will come to an end when the Emperor is taken out of the way, so that he holds up the appearance of the Man of sin no longer.

The true setting of this belief is worked out correctly by Stauffer,[1] who recalls the ancient belief (is it ancient only?) that the forces of Chaos, though temporarily repelled and held at bay by the order of creation, are, as it were, only just outside the door, and are ready at any time to resume control, and flood the universe with disaster. Ordered, civilized existence is a precarious thing, and the supports by which it is underpinned could at any moment be knocked away. There is no doubt that many in the ancient world looked upon the Empire as the means by which they had been delivered from the forces of the underworld, and though historical scholarship can uncover a variety of entirely human motives in Augustus and his successors, there is no need to quarrel with the popular view of them as saviours—at least, if this view is understood within the terms of reference to which it originally applied. Paul's is an application of this evaluation to the terms of Jewish apocalyptic. What the impending break-up of society would mean is described more explicitly elsewhere: wars, earthquakes, famines, pestilence, the disintegration of family life, and so on. Paul concentrates upon the one apocalyptic figure of the Son of perdition. Once the restraining force is removed this figure will be manifested, and no hope remains but the parallel and victorious manifestation of the Lord. How long the Emperor would be permitted to exercise his restraining force is not disclosed, but it seems clear from 1 Thessalonians that Paul believed that the whole eschatological process would be wound up soon.

The Empire, then, operates strictly within this age, but for the restraining of wickedness and vice. The Emperor is God's servant, whether he recognizes the fact or not, and his service is defined in

---

[1] *Theologie des Neuen Testaments* (Geneva 1945), pp. 66f. E.T., *New Testament Theology* (1955), pp. 84f.

terms of the swift eschatological movement of history towards its close. With this observation we may turn to the most famous passage of all, Romans 13.1–7. It has recently been argued by J. Kallas[1] that this paragraph should be regarded as an interpolation, made in a post-Pauline period when the eschatological outlook had lost its urgency, and men found it right—and inevitable—to settle down in this world, and in doing so to achieve a *modus vivendi* with the "powers that be". The theological argument implied here I shall come back to at a later point. On literary grounds the suggestion is not convincing. It is true that there is some textual disorder at the end of the Epistle, but this disorder extends, in the known sources, from the end of chapter 14 to chapter 16; it does not touch chapter 13. It is true that there is no direct connection between 12.21, "Do not be overcome by evil, but overcome evil with good", and 13.1; and that 12.21 would link up well with 13.8, "Owe no man anything—but remember the debt of love you owe one another". But at the end of chapter 12 there are no connections: Paul is stringing together a number of moral exhortations, which are linked only by the fact that they are all manifestations, in different forms, of Christian moral life. "Bless those who persecute you . . ."; "Rejoice with those who rejoice, weep with those who weep . . ."; "Don't be stuck up . . ."; "Don't return evil for evil . . ."; "Live at peace with all men . . ."; "Don't avenge yourselves". This miscellaneous list would justify almost any piece of Christian exhortation as coming next in sequence; we can, however, go further. The last injunction I have quoted—"Don't avenge yourselves"—is followed quite naturally by the contents of 13.1–7. You should not avenge yourselves (*a*) because God will see to vengeance at the Last Day, and (*b*) because, so far as it is necessary and right to anticipate the Last Day, God has arranged for this to be done through the State. At the other end, there is a good connection between 13.7 and 13.8: Render to all what you owe to them (τὰς ὀφειλάς), tribute to whom tribute is due, and so on; and don't forget that you owe to all men the debt of love. Again, it is true that we do not know of any specific reason that might have led Paul to give the Roman Church instruction on its relations with the State; but equally we have no external evidence to tell us why he should have written to Rome about the mutual relations of weak and strong, vegetarians and meat-eaters. In the

[1] *New Testament Studies* 11 (1965), pp. 365–74.

end we cannot say, or expect to be able to say, much more than: Doubtless he had good reason for writing as he did.

Provisionally at least we may take Romans 13.1–7 as Pauline. What does the paragraph say? The central affirmation is that the authority (ἐξουσία) is God's servant (διάκονος, verse 4). From this truth the other propositions of the paragraph follow. As jointly God's servant (διάκονος), the authorities (ἐξουσίαι, or ἄρχοντες) are naturally appointed by God; since they are appointed by God they must be recognized, obeyed, and paid (in taxes). The purpose of the State's service (διακονία) is defined when the authority itself is described as "an instrument of vengeance to carry out God's wrath" (ἔκδικος εἰς ὀργήν). I need not linger over a demonstration that, in Paul's usage, *wrath* (ὀργή) normally suggests the day of wrath—the last judgement; see, for example, Romans 2.5. It is true that there is also a preliminary manifestation of God's wrath (1.18), but this does not alter the primary connotation (though it is not unimportant for the exegesis of our passage). "Instrument of vengeance" (ἔκδικος) has a similar suggestion. Its stem (δικ-) suggests cognate words of the "righteousness" group; and the use of the word itself at 1 Thessalonians 4.6 is worth noting (ἔκδικος κύριος περὶ πάντων τούτων). The cognate *vengeance* (ἐκδίκησις) has just been used (12.19) in a similar sense, and occurs elsewhere, as does the cognate verb, *to avenge* (ἐκδικεῖν). Paul's language suggests the last judgement and the final vengeance upon sinners—as he says in 13.4, upon "the man who practises evil". To execute judgement God confers upon the State appropriate authority; he puts into the magistrate's hand the sword, which he uses to punish the wicked. Thus the State operates, as we have seen, to stem the forces of Chaos, more precisely, to put down those who would disturb the peace of society (correspondingly, though Paul lays little stress on this, to praise those who do well). It does this, moreover, by actually operating the wrath of God. This is seen, on the one hand, in the progressive deterioration of society, in which sin is punished with more sin (1.24, 26, 28), and, on the other, in the State's action to restrain evil. If the State did not take this action, it would be necessary for God to initiate the last judgement at once; that is, the State is seen here to exercise precisely the same restraining, postponing influence as in 2 Thessalonians 2, though here it is looked at from the opposite angle.

It is in the interests of all men to support this activity of the State, and not least of Christians, who must desire not only to be godly and quietly governed, and to avoid, if possible, the terrors of Satan's last rage, but also to have maximum opportunity to publish the gospel. If read in this way Romans 13.1–7 seems to be consistent with Paul's eschatological teaching in general.

I ought, before leaving this passage, to say a word about Oscar Cullmann's well-known view that the "authorities" here are not primarily the State, but the celestial principalities and powers which stand behind and use it. There is much that is attractive in this view; I should agree, for example, that at 1 Corinthians 2.6, 8 the rulers of this age, who, in their ignorance, crucified the Lord of glory, are not rulers such as Pilate and Herod, but the spiritual powers under whose dominion this age runs its course. The strongest objection to Dr Cullmann's interpretation is this. He is right in asserting that God won a decisive victory over principalities and powers in the cross (Col. 2.15), but there is no ground for going on to claim that after their defeat the powers "came in" on God's side as his servants (διάκονοι); on the contrary, they continue to be inimical and to constitute a standing threat to Christians. Thus they cannot be the authorities of God's appointment to whom Christians must be subject. It is the State, as God's appointment for a specific purpose, to which Christians owe this obedience, or subordination. Not that they must obey it, whatever it may command, any more than a wife (of whom the same word is used at Col. 3.18) must obey her husband's order to commit murder; but they must recognize a general relationship of subordination (ὑπο—τάσσεσθαι) on their part, and of superordination on the State's. The State enjoys this superior status in view of the fact that God has delegated to it his judicial function.

In the article to which I have referred, Professor Kallas spoke of a change in the Christian attitude to the State which was due to a fading of the primitive eschatological hope. I believe he is wrong in seeing this change already in Romans 13.1–7, but not wrong in thinking that it eventually took place. The Church could not continue for ever to believe that history—and all political institutions with it—would end within the first generation of Christians. Our next—and last—task must be to sum up the attitude of the first generation, and then consider to what changes it was subjected.

As far as one can see, the main concern of Jesus and the Palestinian Church was not with the foreign secular power, but with apostate Judaism. The secular power was *there*; it was recognized; as long as this world order lasted it had its rights, and its claims should be met—met not only by the payment of taxes, but also by personal service, done willingly, and extending to a second mile. The Church was not its rival, and had no cause to pick a quarrel with it.

For Paul, the State was part of God's providence, designed to keep things going as long as God desired that they should be kept going. It was a bulwark against the forces of darkness, and thus required respect and support. Like the Destroying Angel of 1 Corinthians 10.10 it was an agent of God's judgement, and, as in another context, so no doubt here, Paul would have held that it was better to be disciplined in this world than to be judged in the next (1 Cor. 11.32). The State's function is important, but it is essentially temporary. These views of the State were written down at a time when it was believed that no long future lay ahead, and there had been no serious conflict between Rome and the Christians. We have already noted the relatively simple attitude of Luke, who desired the continuance of these good relations. Rome had never found fault with the Church; on the contrary, it had demonstrated the Church's political innocence. Let the new generation of magistrates take note of the findings of their predecessors, and manifest the same attitude, even if Jews and other trouble-makers try to sow suspicion in their minds.

The Pastoral Epistles, which in many respects reflect the same background and motivation as the Lucan writings, make a similar though not identical point. Christians with appropriate gifts are encouraged to play their part in the leadership of the Christian society, just as their contemporaries were urged to pull their weight in the life of the city-states; the virtues required in Christians, and especially in ministers, are those sought, and honoured, in the good and especially in the prominent citizen; and Christians are urged so to behave as to give no needless cause of offence to heathen with high moral standards (1 Tim. 3.7, 12; 5.10, 14; 6.1; 2 Tim. 2.25f; Titus 1.6f; 2.8; 3.1f, 8f, 14). Luke argues that, historically, the State has no reason to suspect, much less to persecute, the Church; the author of the Pastorals urges Christians to give no unnecessary provocation.

There is much more material in the New Testament—more

than we can at this stage seriously consider. As we begin to look briefly at it, I should like to recall a fact that is often, I think, overlooked by New Testament scholars, who suppose that pronouncements favourable to the State cannot have been written in a time of persecution; or, to put the matter more generally, that the Christian theological estimate of the State was dependent upon the degree of comfort in which Christians were permitted to live. This is, I believe, an illusion. Batiffol has spoken of the *civisme convaincu* of the Church in the first centuries; even when persecuted, Christians knew that they were good citizens, and, notwithstanding occasional injudicious remarks from Tertullian, intended to continue to be good citizens. The incidence of persecution did not greatly affect their attitude to the State.

Thus, though I am favourably disposed to the view that 1 Peter consists of two documents, put together at 4.11, 12 to make one, I do not ground this view, as some do, on the belief that the same author could not in the same document write, "Be in subjection to every human ordinance for the Lord's sake; whether to the king as supreme, or to rulers as sent by him for vengeance [ἐκδίκησις again] upon evildoers and for the praise of those who do good (2.13f) . . . Honour all men, love the brotherhood, fear God, honour the king (2.17)"; and also attest the kind of persecution that appears to underlie chapters 4 and 5. At all events, the editor finally responsible for 1 Peter as we have it appears to have found no difficulty in allowing both pieces of material to stand side by side. In the closing section of the Epistle persecution is ascribed to two causes (which again are not necessarily incompatible): the raging of the devil in the last days, and the disciplinary action of God.

I note this twofold ascription in 1 Peter for its own sake, and also because it provides the necessary introduction to the thought of Revelation, to which, unfortunately, I cannot give the attention it deserves. The thought of this book is often contrasted sharply with that of Paul (and of 1 Pet. 2), since the State (in particular, the Roman State) now appears no longer as God's servant, appointed by him, but as the beast, the agent of the devil. In dealing with this question it is hard to find a middle way between detailed exegesis of all the relevant texts, and the observation of a few essential points which may give some direction to thought on the subject; for this reason, the fact that only the latter course is open to us in the time available may be the less deplored.

The primary New Testament conviction about the State is, as we have seen, that it is one of the provisions made by God for the well-being of his creation. All such providential institutions are open to abuse; elsewhere in the New Testament the abuse of the Law itself is analysed, and it is shown how the holy and spiritual command of God becomes in the hands of sin a weapon by which man, God's creature, is slain. It is perhaps even clearer in the modern than in the ancient world that natural forces, created by God, can be seized and abused. It is this, essentially, that happens to the State, and this that is, one-sidedly perhaps, affirmed in Revelation. Nor is this merely the harnessing of an all-too-willing horse. To retain the metaphor, the horse takes the bit between its teeth and refuses to obey its rider. Other parts of creation—principalities and powers, and, not least, man himself—are represented by the New Testament as being in rebellion against the Creator, and this, according to Revelation, happens to the State; but at its worst the State is a disobedient and rebellious servant, not an abstract and essentially evil being conceived in dualistic terms as standing over against God. Behind these mythological assertions lies the historical fact that, towards the end of the first century, Rome demanded, as it had not previously, the worship of the Emperor as a god. The Emperor was no longer the restraining force who prevented the Man of sin from assuming the role of God; he was the Man of sin, who assumed the role of god and made use of the State as the form of his self-manifestation; and the mythology of Revelation is intended, not to narrate the history of the Empire but to describe this situation.

So far as Revelation sets out to tell a story it is a story of the future—of the things that shall be hereafter; and it is the story that Christians have always told, of the ultimate overthrow of evil and of the sovereignty of God. It was not, however, cast in a form that could be permanently clear and satisfying; the way forward from the New Testament into a Christian dogmatic of something like permanent shape needs the contribution of other Johannine material, to which I have already pointed. There is a kingdom of this world, which receives such authority as it has "from above", and has its own place and function in God's purpose; but there is also a kingdom which is not of this world, which claims the ultimate loyalty and love of the believer. But the story of the two cities, and of the two swords, is one that others must tell.

2

Mark 10.45: A Ransom for Many[1]

This short paper makes no attempt to answer, or even to state, all the historical and theological questions raised by this verse, whose notorious difficulty is known to all students of the New Testament. My intention is to offer one suggestion regarding the background and meaning of one word, λύτρον. Undoubtedly this is a key-word, perhaps the key-word, in the verse, and the suggestion, if it is correct, may well throw some light on the meaning of the verse as a whole, and its place in the Gospel tradition.

It has often been maintained that both the thought and the language of Mark 10.45 are based on the song of the Suffering Servant of the Lord in Isaiah 52.13—53.12. This view has been held both by those who accepted[2] and by those who denied[3] the substantial authenticity of the logion as a saying of Jesus. Those who maintain it usually see in the word λύτρον a reflection of Isaiah 53.10 (*'im-taśim 'aśam napśo*). The LXX translation (ἐὰν δῶτε περὶ ἁμαρτίας, ἡ ψυχὴ ὑμῶν. . .) differs somewhat, but renders *'aśam* correctly enough by περὶ ἁμαρτίας. I have argued elsewhere[4] that the literary connection between Mark 10.45 and Isaiah 53 is neither proved nor capable of proof. Verbal contact between *'aśam* and λύτρον does not exist,[5] and without such contact the argument that λύτρον and *'aśam* are both to be understood "in der übertragenen Bedeutung 'Ersatzzahlung'"[6] ("in the

---

[1] Originally one of the collection of essays presented to Professor G. Delling, of Halle, in honour of his sixty-fifth birthday, 10 May 1970.

[2] For example, V. Taylor, *Commentary* ad loc.

[3] For example, E. Haenchen, *Der Weg Jesu* (1966), p. 369.

[4] "The Background of Mark 10.45", in *New Testament Essays: Studies in Memory of T. W. Manson*, ed. A. J. B. Higgins (1959), pp. 1–18; cf. M. D. Hooker, *Jesus and the Servant* (1959), pp. 74–9; *The Son of Man in Mark* (1967), pp. 140–7.

[5] *'aśam* is never, in the Greek Old Testament, rendered by λύτρον or any of its cognates; none of the Hebrew words that λύτρον and its cognates represent occurs in Isa. 53.

[6] E. Lohse, *Märtyrer und Gottesknecht* (1955), p. 119.

transferred sense of 'substitutionary payment'") can hardly carry conviction.

The belief that Mark in this verse is simply reproducing a piece of Pauline theology is now for the most part abandoned; λύτρον is not a Pauline word.[1] To say, however, that Mark 10.45 is not Pauline is by no means to end the discussion. The saying has been attributed to the early Hellenistic communities,[2] to the Palestinian Church,[3] and to Jesus himself.[4] Whether or not Jesus spoke it, it undoubtedly evolved into the theology of the Hellenistic Church, as 1 Timothy 2.6 is enough to prove, and notwithstanding the Hellenistic character of Luke 22.24ff[5] the absence of a parallel to the λύτρον saying in Luke 22.27 cannot fail to throw its antiquity into question. If the saying is not to be regarded as allusion to, or exegesis of, Isaiah 53.10, we are bound to ask what kind of origin or impulse can have given rise to the tradition. That the early Church believed in the atoning power and the representative efficacy of the death of Jesus is certain, and it is certain too that the formulation of this belief developed with the general development of Christian theology. But from what historical origin?

The linguistic relations of λύτρον and its cognates have often been sketched[6] and call for no more than brief summary here. In the LXX λυτροῦν translates

1. (a) ge'ullah (b) ga'al
2. koper
3. mᵉhir
4. (a) pidyon (b) padah qal. (c) ho. (d) pᵉduy (e) pidyom.[7]

Consideration of λυτροῦν, λύτρωσις, λυτρωτής, and λυτρωτός, adds little on the Hebrew side. p-l-ṭ is hardly worth noticing on the strength of Psalm 31 (32).7; p-ṣ-h on the strength of Psalm 143 (144).10; and so on. The only roots of real importance are g-'-l,

---

[1] Though ἀπολύτρωσις is (Rom. 3.24; 8.23; 1 Cor. 1.30; cf. Eph. 1.7, 14; 4.30; Col. 1.14), and the ἀντίλυτρον ὑπὲρ πάντων of 1 Tim. 2.6, though not written by Paul, probably developed in Pauline Churches.

[2] R. Bultmann, *Die Geschichte der synoptischen Tradition* (1931), p. 154; in the *Ergänzungsheft* (1962) he maintains his view against E. Lohse, J. Jeremias, and H. W. Wolff.

[3] E. Lohse, op. cit., pp. 116–22; it is 10.45b, the saying about the λύτρον, that is in question here.

[4] J. Jeremias on παῖς θεοῦ in *TWNT* 5, p. 713.

[5] E. Lohse, op. cit., p. 119.

[6] See especially O. Procksch and F. Büchsel in *TWNT* 4, pp. 329–59.

[7] The data are taken from Hatch–Redpath, 890.

k-p-r, *m-ḥ-r*, and *p-d-h*, and of these the third can safely be neglected. The other three roots all suggest the payment of a ransom-price on behalf of others, or for the benefit of others; of the possible nouns *kop̄er* is the most common and in most respects the most suitable; it is not surprising that Delitzsch uses it at Mark 10.45[1] in his translation of the New Testament into Hebrew. But what exactly does it mean, and how did it come to be used? Part of the answer is to be found in the notion that the suffering of the martyrs had atoning efficacy;[2] it seems to me, however, that it is possible to add to this suggestion, to make it more precise, and to say something about its original setting and subsequent development.

Also derived from the root *k-p-r*, another noun, *kapparah*,[3] occurs in a rabbinic turn of speech that is attested from time to time[4] as a more or less conventional expression, indicating a measure of sympathy or attachment more or less sincerely felt.[5] This may be used with reference to an individual; for example, at Qiddushin 31 b it is laid down that a man introducing an opinion of his father's should not say simply

"Thus said my father", but "Thus said my father, my master (*mari*)—May I be an expiation for his rest (*hᵃreni kapparaṯ miškᵉḇo*)!" This is done within twelve months [of his death]. Afterwards he must say, "May his memory be for a blessing, for the life of the world to come!"

Here the relationship is personal; it may also be public. Sanhedrin 2.1 deals with the duties and privileges of the High Priest in various circumstances. If he suffers bereavement,

When he receives comfort from others, all the people say to him, "May we be an expiation for you (*'anu kapparaṯᵉḵa*)", and he replies, "Be ye blessed of heaven."

Other personal references may be found at Sukkah 20a and Yoma

---

[1] Also (and with *nap̄šo* for ἑαυτόν) at 1 Tim. 2.6.
[2] See my article referred to on p. 20, n. 4; also *Jesus and the Gospel Tradition* (1967), pp. 40–5. Relevant though requiring modification is also A. Schweitzer's view that Jesus resolved to take upon himself the whole of the messianic affliction, that the rest of men might go free.
[3] Used by Delitzsch at 1 John 2.2; 4.10 to translate ἱλασμός.
[4] Strack-Billerbeck 3, p. 261, "der nicht seltene Ausruf".
[5] "Loquendi modus, quo loquens utitur ad testandum magnitudinem amoris sui"; Buxtorf, s.v.

23a. Similar words are used of Israel as a whole. Thus at Midrash R. Esther 13a, on Esther 1.11 (To bring Vashti before the king with the royal crown),

> R. Aibo said, "May I be an expiation for Israel (*kapparaṭan šel yiśra'el*); as Israel were eating and drinking and rejoicing, they were blessing and praising and lauding the Holy One, blessed be he! . . .

How formalized and empty the expression could become is illustrated by Negaim 2.1:

> R. Ishmael says: "The children of Israel, may I be an expiation for them ('*ani kapparaṭan*), are like boxwood, neither black nor white, but of the intermediate shade.

This is a sufficiently vapid form of the sentiment, which appears to have been retained in modern Hebrew.[1] It would, however, be quite wrong to suppose that the origin of the expression was merely conventional and void of real meaning. The opposite is probably true. Phrases tend to lose their original force (and sometimes their linguistic preciseness) in the course of time. One thinks, for example, of the conventional English "Goodbye", which today very seldom retains its original meaning of "God be with you". It is probable that "May I be an expiation for Israel" was at first seriously and indeed passionately meant. This can be affirmed because we know the origin of the phrase, which certainly looks back to Moses' desire to make atonement for Israel after the sin of the Golden Calf.

> You have sinned a great sin; but now I will go up to the Lord. Perhaps I shall make atonement (*'akapperah*) for your sin (Exod. 32.30).

The willingness of Moses to be blotted out of God's book on behalf of his people made a great impression on readers of the Pentateuch, and the voluntary self-sacrifice (or readiness for self-sacrifice) of other Old Testament figures was sometimes described in terms of it. Before the phrase descended to the level of conventional piety and politeness, men must have used it to express

---

[1] R. Sivan and E. A. Levenston, *The Megiddo Modern Dictionary*, Hebrew–English, p. 338: "*ḥareni kapparato*, let my life be an expiatory sacrifice for him (an expression of love)".

their devotion, either to their people as a whole, or to their family or some other section of Israel.

It is suggested here that behind the statement in Mark 10.45, that the Son of man came to give his life as a λύτρον ἀντὶ πολλῶν, there lies a use of the phrase in which Jesus expressed his devotion —a devotion that would shrink from no sacrifice—to the true welfare of his people, the "many" (πολλοί, *rabbim*). If this expression is to be given any but the widest connotation, it will point not at all in a Qumranite, or quasi-Qumranite, direction,[1] but towards the *'amme ha'areṣ*, the great mass of the people as opposed to (though not in this case necessarily excluding) the pious groups. The mission of Jesus was to Israel as a whole,[2] but in the circumstances of the time this meant a special emphasis upon those who otherwise were neglected; this is reflected in, for example, Mark 2.17; Luke 19.10.

A saying of this kind could originally have been quite open; that is, it need have had no specific reference to the death of the speaker, but only the general sense, "I would do anything for my people". There are, however, two reasons why it should have tended towards a special connection with death.

(a) Especially if it was cast in a form including the word *nepeš* (and Mark 10.45 as it stands includes ψυχή)[3] used with the meaning "myself", the sense of life—life given up in death— was near at hand. Compare Mark 8.34, where it is hard to know whether to translate τὴν ψυχὴν αὐτοῦ as "himself" or "his life".

(b) Historically—and this is a more important point—the devotion of Jesus to the religious outcasts of Israel contributed very considerably to his death. This, with the implied criticism of the law, brought him into conflict with the authorities of his people.

Once the connection with the death of Jesus was made the saying would inevitably be exposed to theological polishing. Comparison of Mark 10.41-5 with the partial parallel in Luke 22.25-7 not only shows that such polishing has taken place but also that the two

---

[1] Denoting a closed community. See the excellent note of H. Braun, *Qumran und das Neue Testament* II (1966), p. 334.

[2] E. Schweizer, *Church Order in the New Testament* (1961), §2a.

[3] Delitzsch has *napšo* at 1 Tim. 2.6.

Gospels contain independent traditions.[1] Each has some features that are more primitive than the other. The theological development was not all on Hellenistic soil. Passages cited by Schlatter[2] illustrate not only the theological use of *kapparah* and its cognates but also the use of *nepeš* just mentioned, in a sense somewhere between the simple reflexive, which is already common in biblical Hebrew,[3] and "life". The purpose of the present note is not to deny the existence of this theological development of the tradition, but to suggest a possible starting-point, itself of both historical and theological significance, for the tradition. If Jesus did not say, I am (or, My soul is) a *kapparah* for all Israel, he acted on this principle, and this service to the mass of his people occasioned, and at the same time provided the interpretation of, his death.

A note should be added on Sotah 14a, which connects the intercession of Moses (Exod. 32.30ff) with Isaiah 53. The passage runs as follows:

> Rabbi Simlai taught: Why did Moses our teacher express the desire to enter into the land of Israel? Was it because he needed to eat of its fruits, or because he needed to enjoy its good things? No; but this is what Moses said: Many commandments have been given to Israel which cannot be kept except in the land of Israel. I will enter into the land in order that they all may be kept by me. The Holy One, blessed be he, said to him: You are only seeking this in order to receive reward. I will reckon it to you as though you had kept them, as it is written, Therefore will I divide him a portion with the great, and he shall divide the spoil with the strong; because he poured out his soul unto death, and was numbered with the transgressors: yet he bare the sin of many, and made intercession for the transgressors (Isa. 53.12). "Therefore will I divide him a portion with the great"—perhaps with the later but not with the earlier? But the text says, "He shall divide the spoil with the strong", like Abraham, Isaac, and Jacob, who were strong in the Torah and the commandments, "because he poured out his soul unto death", for he gave himself up to death, as it is written, Yet now, if thou wilt forgive their sin—; and if not, blot me, out of thy book which thou hast

---

[1] E. Lohse, op. cit., p. 118; H. E. Tödt, *Der Menschensohn in der synoptischen Überlieferung* (1959), p. 187.

[2] *Der Evangelist Matthäus* (1948), p. 602.

[3] Brown, Driver, Briggs, *Lexicon* s.v.

C

written (Exod. 32.32). "He was numbered with the transgressors", for he was counted with those who died in the wilderness; "yet he bare the sin of many", for he made expiation (*kipper*) for their deed with the calf; "and he made intercession for the transgressors", for he sought for mercy for the transgressors of Israel, that they might return in penitence. Intercession is nothing other than prayer, as it is written, Pray not thou for this people, neither lift up cry nor prayer for them, neither make intercession to me (Jer. 7.16).

This connection might seem to bring back the interpretation of Mark 10.45 to the Suffering Servant of the Lord of Isaiah 53, but in fact it is not so. Rabbi Simlai's interpretation was almost certainly motivated by anti-Christian polemic.[1] If Christians used Isaiah 53 of their Messiah, he would show that it properly applied to, and was fulfilled in, Moses.

[1] J. Jeremias, *TWNT* 5, pp. 684f.

3

The Prologue of St John's Gospel

In this study I propose to direct attention to one passage in the Bible, and attempt to make some contribution to our understanding of it. No one will complain that the passage, the first eighteen verses of the Fourth Gospel, is unworthy of concentrated study. From the time when, with what looks like an odd reluctance, the Gospel emerged into public use in the second century, these verses, more even than the rest of this much studied book, have been at the centre of exegetical and theological debate. Irenaeus of Lyons made substantial use of them in his polemic against the Gnostics, though he was well aware of the fact that the same Gnostics were able to use the same verses for their own purposes; and precisely the same situation is neatly illustrated by Clement of Alexandria's *Extracts from (the Gnostic) Theodotus*. Clement and the Valentinians alike draw heavily on the Prologue to establish their positions. Augustine in a very famous passage in the *Confessions* (7.9.1f) puts his finger on the spot when he points out, perhaps not quite accurately, that much of the Prologue is to be found in Platonic writings, but adds, "But that the Word became flesh, and dwelt among us, I did not read there . . . those books do not have it." Augustine has long been followed in finding in verse 14, "The Word became flesh", the centre and climax of the Prologue; we shall see reason at least to question this view—it may be that Augustine was thinking as an ex-Manichaean. What is hardly open to question is the universal instinct of Christendom, which has found here the climax of New Testament Christology, itself the edge of the New Testament message.

If we are to follow Irenaeus, Clement, Augustine, and many another in Christian history, in seeing in John's Prologue a focal point of biblical theology and a foundation of Christian doctrine, we must also recognize that our age has studied the Prologue in a new way. Clement's Valentinians, for example, identified John's

Beginning and *Only-begotten*; the Word was in the Beginning, in the Only-begotten, and as Word and Life could be identified with Christ: they brought with them their own conception of a *pleroma* of spiritual, celestial beings, and made what identifications they could. Augustine took the Word in John to be the same Word he had encountered in "certain books of the Platonists, translated from Greek into Latin". Today we are humble enough to recognize that we too, as we approach Scripture, are not without presuppositions, but at least we are aware of the fact and do our best not to let them run away with us. If we cannot shake ourselves free of our own historical environment, at least we do our best to concentrate on John's. This concentration naturally involves consideration of what John meant by the term Word and of the background whence he drew it: Were its roots in the Old Testament or Greek philosophy? in gnosis or in Judaism? or in some combination of these? But it involves also the question : By what literary and theological processes did the Prologue come to be what we now read? Did John simply write it out as the thoughts occurred to him? Or was there some literary foundation on which he worked, a source he took over, remodelled, supplemented, glossed? This is a question that has been to some extent by-passed by recent English commentators, who have for the most part been content to take the Prologue—and the rest of the Gospel, for that matter—as it stands and not to concern themselves with sources—often, indeed, to maintain that the Gospel is so closely woven that it is impossible to detect seams and joins in its texture. Hoskyns and Lightfoot, Dodd, Sanders, and Marsh—there is little of the analysis that we read in Bultmann, Käsemann, and Haenchen to be found here. This seems a pity. I am not saying that the non-analysts are wrong; we shall return to the question who is right and who is wrong at a later point; but I think they may have overlooked a useful tool. The purpose of analysis was laid down in classical terms by Bultmann:[1] "Of course, exegesis has to explain the complete text, and the critical analysis exists in order to serve this explanation." This vital definition has, I suspect, been sometimes forgotten, or overlooked, on both sides. The non-analysts have forgotten that analysis can serve their laudable intention of expounding the entire canonical text, and the analysts have forgotten that exegesis must in the end concern itself with this entire text

---

[1] *Das Evangelium des Johannes* (Göttingen 1950), p. 4.

and contented themselves with reconstructing a primitive form, an *Urprolog*, of which the canonical text is an inferior, bowdlerized version, which can be safely consigned to the historical museum.

I have spoken of analysis, and quoted the word from Bultmann. What does it mean? It turns upon those theological and literary questions I referred to a few moments ago. They apply to the whole Gospel, but they are concentrated in the Prologue, and this will certainly provide us with problems enough. It is important to see that the theological and literary questions belong together. It is not enough to ask in general terms, What is the religious environment of the Gospel? and to hunt out in Greek, Jewish, and Iranian literature the use of such terms as Word, Light, Life, Only-begotten. This is part of the task, but we must also trace out, so far as we can, the movement of John's thought from verse to verse, and from clause to clause, looking out for breaks or weak links in the argument, for joins and leaps. Purely literary questions of form must be considered too; we shall see in a moment that many recent students of the question believe the Prologue to have been written originally in verse, in which a few passages stand out as incongruous and inharmonious prose. If this observation is correct, it provides a powerful analytical tool. We must ask also how the Prologue is related to the Gospel as a whole. Some think of the Prologue as the staple Johannine proposition, illustrated at length in the narratives and discourses that follow; others think that the Prologue was written as an introductory summary, based on the main substance of the book. For myself, I suspect that this is a chicken-and-egg problem. The Gospel was surely intended to be read many times—there is no other way to understand it; and after the first reading the process is a circular one. The next time I read the Prologue I shall read it in the light of my knowledge of the whole book; and when I go on to read the rest of the book, I shall read it in the light of my knowledge of the Prologue. Still, the question must be raised, and raised in an analytical, critical way. Does the Prologue really introduce the Gospel as we know it? Could it have existed, did it at one time exist, independently of the Gospel?

These generalities are perhaps not illuminating; it will be more useful to give specific examples of analysis. The present generation in this as in other matters stands on the shoulders of its predecessors, and the work of our predecessors is best represented by

J. H. Bernard[1] and C. F. Burney.[2] I know no account of the matter clearer and more succinct than Bernard's, and it will in the end save time if I quote him at length.

The hymn is a philosophical *rationale* of the main thesis of the Gospel. It begins with the proclamation of the Word as Pre-existent and Divine (vv. 1, 2). Then appear the O.T. thoughts of the Word as creative of all (v. 3), life-giving (v. 4), light-giving (v. 5). But the whole universe (v. 10), including man (v. 11), was unconscious of His omnipresent energy. He became Incarnate, not as a momentary Epiphany of the Divine, but as an abiding and visible exhibition of the Divine Glory, even as the Son exhibits the Father (v. 14). Thus does the Word as Incarnate reveal the Invisible God (v. 18).

Two parenthetical notes as to the witness of John the Baptist, to the coming Light (vv. 6–9), and His pre-existence (v. 15), are added. We have also two exegetical comments by the evangelist, at vv. 12, 13, to correct the idea which v. 11 might convey, that no one received or recognised the Word when He came; and again at vv. 16, 17, to illustrate the "grace and truth" of v. 14.

The great theme of a Divine Revealer of God is implicit in the first and last stanzas of the hymn (vv. 1, 18), the rest being concerned with the method of the revelation.

The Hebraic style of the hymn is plain. The repetition in the second line of a couplet of what has been said already in the first line (vv. 3, 5); the elucidation of the meaning of the first line by the emphatic word being repeated in the next (vv. 4, 5, 11, 14), which provides an illustration of what has been called "climactic parallelism" (cf. Ps. 29.5; 93.3); the threefold repetition in the first three lines of v. 14, all of which involve the bodily visibility of the Logos—sufficiently show that the model is not Greek but Hebrew poetry.

It will be noticed that the hymn moves in abstract regions of thought. The historical names—John, Moses, Jesus Christ—are no part of it: they are added in the explanatory notes of the evangelist. Nevertheless, v. 14 states an historical fact and points to an event in time; but the history is told *sub specie aeternitatis* (p. cxlv).

---

[1] *A Critical and Exegetical Commentary on the Gospel according to St. John* (1928).

[2] *The Aramaic Origin of the Fourth Gospel* (1922).

This produces a Prologue-source made up as follows: 1, 2, 3, 4, 5, 10, 11, 14, 18. John's additions to it have to some extent changed its character. C. F. Burney's reconstructed source ran in couplets as follows: 1a1b; 1c2a; 3a3b; 4a4b; 5a5b; 10b10c; 11a11b; 14a14b; 14c14d; 14e16a; 17a17b. This is similar to Bernard's selection, but not identical with it. Both retain 1–5; both omit 6–9; Burney drops 10a, which Bernard retains; both retain 11, but drop 12 and 13; both retain 14, and omit 15. Thereafter they diverge: Bernard omits 16, 17, but retains 18; Burney includes 16a, 17, but omits the rest. There is a further important difference, in that whereas Bernard is content to describe his source rather vaguely as "Hebraic", Burney sets out to prove in detail that his was written originally in Aramaic couplets.

In the analysis of the Prologue no one has more subtly combined purely formal considerations with considerations based on content than R. Bultmann.[1] The end result does not differ widely from Bernard's, but the argumentation is closer, and Bultmann sees in the source of the Prologue as he reconstructs it part of the *Offenbarungsreden* (Revelation discourses), the source which he believes to underlie the discourse material in the Gospel as a whole. The "chain" or "step" form of parallelism carries one through the first five verses, where one line is linked with the next by the repetition of a word; for example,

> In the beginning was *the Word*,
> And *the Word* was with God.

It is true that verse 2 is only doubtfully supported by this observation, and may not come from the source. Verse 9 (which neither Bernard nor Burney would have in his source) is linked with verse 10 by the word *world*; 11a and b are linked by *own*, 11 and 12 by *receive*, 14a and b by *glory*, 14b and 16 by *full—fullness*. Already it appears that verses 6, 7, 8, 13, 15 disturb the sequence. So much for formal, literary analysis. Study of the contents, of the line of thought, of the Prologue leads to a similar conclusion. The turning-point of the Prologue is verse 14, which speaks of the incarnation of the Logos: the Word became flesh. Up to this point,

---

[1] In addition to the Commentary (note 1 on p. 28) see especially "Der religionsgeschichtliche Hintergrund des Prologs zum Johannes-Evangelium", *EYXAPIΣTHPION, Festschrift Hermann Gunkel* (Göttingen 1923), 2, pp. 3–26.

therefore, we must have been dealing with the pre-existent Logos. In the first five verses this is clear enough; but what of verse 11 ("he came to his own home") which appears to refer to the historical coming of Christ to Israel? But it is verses 6–8 that make verse 11 refer to an historical event, ~~the ministry of Jesus ushered in by the testimony of the Baptist;~~ leave out verses 6–8, and verse 11 will refer back to verses 3, 4, and in consequence take on a different meaning, ~~no longer determined by the historical reference to John the Baptist but by the eternal~~ being and properties of the Logos. By arguments such as these Bultmann arrives at a source constituted as follows: 1, (2), 3, 4, 5, 9, (10a), 10b c, 11, 12, 14, 16.

He accepts Burney's theory of an Aramaic origin for the source as he reconstructs it, and uses it to save the poetic character of the material where it might otherwise disappear. Thus in verse 12, "He gave them authority to become children of God", the word *authority* is superfluous to the rhythm; it was added, Bultmann thinks, when the Semitic idiom, "He gave to become", that is, "he caused to become", was turned into Greek. But what is specially to be noted in Bultmann's work is the combination of literary and theological analysis. This has been, on the whole, continued by those who have been critical of Bultmann's work.

Of these, the only one whose work I can attempt even briefly to summarize is E. Käsemann.[1] On the literary side, Käsemann differs from Bultmann on two major points. He considers that the Aramaic origin of the material in the Prologue has not been demonstrated with sufficient cogency to justify the use which (as we have just seen) Bultmann makes of it. It cannot be used, for example, to save the poetic structure of verse 12; and the same is true of verse 9. This means that these two verses immediately fall under suspicion as supplements to the original poetical Prologue. And, secondly, Käsemann observes that the formal characteristics (especially step parallelism) that are so marked in verses 1–5 do not recur, at least to anything like the same extent, in verses 14–18. There is thus a prima facie literary case for separating verses 14–18 from the earlier part of the Prologue, and this observation will lead to Käsemann's most important theological dispute with Bultmann. Before we reach the theology, however, two further observations are called for. Verse 13 is to be excluded from the source on account

---

[1] "Aufbau und Anliegen des johanneischen Prologs" in *Exegetische Versuche und Besinnungen* II (Göttingen 1964), pp. 155–80.

of its prose style—it is a prose gloss on the meaning of regeneration; and verse 9 is an insertion designed to link the interpolated John the Baptist material (like Bernard, and most students, Käsemann regards verses 6–8 as no part of the original Prologue) with the main theme—by denying explicitly that the Baptist is the Light it becomes possible to return to the Logos who is the true Light. There is now not very much of the Prologue left. What remains may be divided into two strophes. The first consists of seven lines (or eight, if verse 2 is included): 1a, 1b, 1c, (2), 3a, 3b, 4a, 4b; and the second consists of seven lines: 5a, 5b, 10a, 10b, 10c, 11a, 11b. Of verse 12 Käsemann says that it may be regarded as the "crown of the whole".[1] This comment is intended, I suppose, to be taken both formally—a couplet rounding off the two strophes—and theologically. The movement of thought is completed by the rebirth of believers as the children of God.

This analysis provides the key to the evangelist's intention and thus to the theological interpretation of the Prologue. The evangelist's most important editorial action is to provide the hymn as he found it with a postscript consisting of verses 14–18. From this observation two deductions are drawn.

1 Since the hymn—which Käsemann believes to have been already Christian before John edited it—was already complete with verse 12, there must have been before this point a reference to the incarnation, or rather to the entry of the Logos into the world; apart from the "became flesh" of verse 14 there is no specific justification for speaking of this entry as *incarnation*. The entry is to be found in the second strophe, in verses 5, 10, 11. "The verb in verse 5 is not timeless, but, as in the excellent parallel in 1 John 2.8, has the ring of the present".[2]

2 Since the decisive entry of the Logos into the world has already been dealt with before verse 14 is reached, this entry cannot be the main theme of verse 14. Bultmann (and, *mutatis mutandis*, one could add the name of Augustine, and not a few others) therefore is wrong in laying so much stress upon the paradox and offence of "the Word became flesh", of the assertion that the Revealer appeared in stark humanity. It was not John's intention to underline this paradox. The assertion that the Word became flesh does not mean the proposition—startling and paradoxical enough in a

[1] Op. cit., p. 168.   [2] Ibid., p. 166.

gnostic context—that the revelation was veiled under the cloak of human existence, but rather that the revelation found appropriate means of becoming visible, of communicating itself. The stress lies not here but on the next clause, "We beheld his glory". The way is open, one may remark, for the Johannine docetism which Käsemann argues more fully in his book[1] on John 17.

Time forbids me to go into more detail, or to cast the net wider. Those who desire more detail must go to the books and articles, those who desire a wider sweep to the commentaries of R. E. Brown[2] and R. Schnackenburg.[3] These two authors, in addition to providing valuable summaries of the views of others, have their own reconstructions of the Prologue source. Brown, for example, envisages a source of four strophes:

1. 1, 2   The Word with God
2. 3–5   The Word and creation
3. 10–12b   The Word in the world
4. 14, 16   The community's share in the Word.

The remaining pieces, supplements made at later stages, are the following:

1. 12c–13   added to explain how men become God's children
2. 17, 18   added to explain "love in place of love" ($\chi \acute{\alpha} \rho \iota \nu$ $\dot{\alpha} \nu \tau \grave{\iota}$ $\chi \acute{\alpha} \rho \iota \tau o s$, verse 16)
3. 6–9, 15   material about John the Baptist, perhaps originally the opening verses of the Gospel, displaced when the Prologue was added.

Schnackenburg finds the original Prologue in verses 1, 3, 4, 9, 10, 11, 14, 16 (with the omission of a few words).

I have given so much detail (and wish I could have given more) partly as a point of departure for a somewhat different treatment, and partly because I believe (as I have said) that the work of such men as Bultmann, Käsemann, Haenchen,[4] and Schnackenburg has been neglected to the impoverishment of current English work on John. This does not mean that I think it should be blindly fol-

---

[1] *Jesu letzter Wille nach Johannes 17* (Tübingen 1966). E.T., *The Testament of Jesus: a Study of the Gospel of St John in the light of Chapter 17* (1968).

[2] *The Gospel according to John (i–xii)* (New York 1966).

[3] *The Gospel according to St John*, vol. 1 (1968).

[4] "Probleme des johanneischen Prologs" in *Zeitschrift für Theologie und Kirche* 60 (1963), pp. 305–34.

lowed; far from it. We have much to learn from it, especially from the rigorous discussion of the line of thought that runs through the Prologue—with, or without, interruptions. But my next step is to challenge two widely held critical views about the background of the Prologue.

The first is the Aramaic origin of the Prologue (or of the original parts of it). This is indeed not a universally held opinion. We have seen that it was maintained by Burney and Bultmann. It was denied by Käsemann, who in this is joined by J. Jeremias.[1] Brown makes no attempt to settle the question; "the evidence is not conclusive".[2] A study of this kind is hardly the place for detailed linguistic discussion, and a few observations must suffice. None of the alleged Semitisms is convincing; an equally convincing, or more convincing, explanation that does not resort to a hypothetical Aramaic original can be found in every case, and there are several sentences that are undoubtedly Greek rather than Semitic in conception. An outstanding example of this is to be found in verse 11 (universally, I think, allowed to be part of the original Prologue), where the evangelist says that the Word came to his own home (τὰ ἴδια, neuter plural), and his own people (οἱ ἴδιοι, masculine plural) did not receive him. This variation in gender cannot be expressed in Aramaic (which can only use *dileh* in each case). It is worth noting that the Syriac New Testament quite fails to make John's point here. In the next verse commentators have been exercised by the statement that to believers the Word gave authority to become (ἔδωκεν ἐξουσίαν γενέσθαι) children of God. Bultmann (as we have seen) wished to excise "authority", which he thinks spoils the rhythm, as a Greek addition to the Semitic idiom "he gave to become", that is, "he caused to become"; others have seen in ἐξουσία followed by the infinitive a Semitic turn of speech. It is in fact neatly paralleled by the plain Greek of *Corpus Hermeticum* 1.28: "Having authority to partake (ἐξουσίαν . . . μεταλαβεῖν) of immortality". The use of periphrastic tenses, and of *casus pendens*, is by no means exclusively Semitic.

The Prologue as a whole is written in extremely simple Greek, Greek so simple that it seems almost naïve. This has been regarded as a mark of Semitic origin, but it is not so. Greek is indeed capable

---

[1] *The Central Message of the New Testament* (1965), p. 74: "almost certainly composed in Greek".
[2] Op. cit., p. 23.

of the utmost refinement and complication; but not every Greek was a Thucydides, and there is also very simple Greek. I have in mind not so much the personal letters of the papyri as that solemn, religious, hieratic Greek, to be found in some inscriptions, in religious and magical papyri, and in literature such as the Hermetica. The language of the Prologue belongs to this category; it is not necessarily Semitic because it is simple.

The second widely held view that I propose to query is that the Prologue, at least in its primitive form, was written in verse. This proposition has been so frequently repeated that it is almost universally accepted without question. It is true that Haenchen speaks of "free rhythms", but without denying that verse of a kind is used, and when J. N. Sanders says that "the Prologue is written in rhythmical prose, though it does not seem possible to arrange it in any generally acceptable metrical scheme"[1] he does not develop the point in relation to critical reconstructions. It is a point well worth developing.

I had occasion long ago to point out[2] that Burney and J. Weiss give quite different reconstructions of the supposed poetical source. Käsemann has retorted[3] that an observation of this kind is not an adequate refutation of the general theory that such a source once existed. In this he is quite right, and I never supposed that merely to point out the disagreement was logically a disproof. It is possible that Burney was right and Weiss wrong; it is possible that Burney was wrong and Weiss right; it is possible that both were wrong, and yet that a poetic structure that escaped them both was in fact there. Logical refutation was not and is not the point; the point is that when scholars of such distinction as Burney and Weiss look at the same material, and one of them describes it as poetry and the other as prose, one begins to question their terms, their definitions, and the distinctions they are attempting to draw. This doubt is increased when one looks at the instructive table on p. 22 of Brown's Commentary, where the views of eight scholars (Bernard, Bultmann, De Ausejo, Gaechter, Green, Haenchen, Käsemann, Schnackenburg) are set out. If we combine their views, a maximum of thirteen verses are ascribed to the poetic source

---

[1] *The Gospel according to St John*, edited and completed by B. A. Mastin (1968), p. 67.

[2] In *The Gospel according to St John* (1955), p. 126.

[3] "Aufbau und Anliegen", p. 162.

(1–5, 9–12, 14, 16–18); the minimum figure, of verses which all are agreed in ascribing to the poetic source, is five (1, 3, 4, 10, 11). The list includes the names of some of the greatest living New Testament scholars; yet in this instance they do not appear to be much clearer about the distinction between prose and verse than Molière's Bourgeois Gentilhomme.

What in fact is meant by verse in this context? In any other field of Greek literature we should know precisely what was meant by verse. Greek verse is an art-form that follows very precise prosodical rules, which are based not upon stress but upon quantity; it consists, that is, of regular patterns of long and short syllables. It is immediately evident that there is no verse of this kind in John's Prologue, no regular configuration of quantity. When it is claimed that the Prologue is written in, or based on, verse, a different kind of verse is in mind—radically different, since, like the verse that recent generations of scholars have detected in the Old Testament, it is based not on quantity but on stress. But were the Greeks aware of the existence of this kind of verse? The answer to this question is, I think, No; not even Hellenistic Jews seem to have been aware of it. Josephus, for example, knew that according to the Torah Moses had uttered songs, but in order to give to Greek readers the right impression he was obliged to describe the songs of Exodus 15 and Deuteronomy 32 as written in hexameters;[1] similarly he knew that David must be described as the composer of songs and hymns, and said that he wrote in various measures, sometimes trimeter, sometimes pentameter.[2] Nothing could be further from the truth; but nothing else would have conveyed anything like the right idea to a Greek. We may compare Philo's account of the hymns of the Therapeutae; these, he says, were in all kinds of metres, "hexameters and iambics, lyrics suitable for processions or in libations and at the altars, or for the chorus whilst standing or dancing, with careful metrical arrangements to fit the various evolutions".[3]

Hellenistic Jews, and Christians too, may well have used Greek metres on occasion; they probably also used prose. Antiquity in general found no difficulty in singing prose, and this is what early Christian hymns, from "O gladsome Light" to the *Te Deum*, for the most part were. This means that the only way in which the

---

[1] *Antiquities* 2. 346; 4. 303.   [2] Ibid., 7. 305.
[3] *De Vita Contemplativa* 29, 80; F. H. Colson's translation.

poetic structure—in any serious sense of the adjective—of the Prologue can be saved is to maintain that it represents not Greek but Semitic verse, based not on quantity but on stress; and five reasons make it very difficult to believe this.

(*a*) The Hebrew verse of the Old Testament was "discovered" by Robert Lowth in 1753 (the date of his *De Sacra Poesi Hebraeorum Praelectiones Academicae*); most earlier users of Hebrew, for example in the New Testament period, do not seem to have been aware of it. Prose and verse, notably the Shema, the Eighteen Benedictions, and the Hallel Psalms, were all sung in the synagogue in the same way.[1]

(*b*) As we have already seen, Josephus and Philo did not recognize what we call Hebrew verse as having a distinctive pattern and principle of its own.

(*c*) Nor did the LXX translators, who "seem to have no sense of rhythm",[2] recognize this. When, exceptionally, it was recognized, apparently by the translators of Proverbs, and perhaps of Job, they showed their recognition not by reproducing the form of the Hebrew verse but by including rough hexameter and iambic lines.[3]

(*d*) Most important of all is the fact I have already mentioned though I have in this study no time to demonstrate it: that the case for a Semitic original of the Prologue will not stand.

(*e*) Completing the inference to be drawn from this is the fact that we can see how from time to time Greek prose falls into a form which, if it occurred in Scripture, might easily be claimed as both poetic and Semitic. Of this I cite as an example the great hymn at the end of the Poimandres (*Corpus Hermeticum* 1.31f):

Holy is God, the Father of all things.
Holy is God, whose will is performed by his own powers.
Holy is God, who wills to be known, and is known to his own.
Holy art thou, who by the Logos hast constituted what exists.
Holy art thou, of whom all nature has become the image.
Holy art thou, whom nature did not form.

---

[1] H. L. Strack and P. Billerbeck, *Kommentar zum Neuen Testament aus Talmud und Midrasch* (Munich 1922–61), vol. 4, p. 394.

[2] H. B. Swete, *An Introduction to the Old Testament in Greek*, revised by R. R. Ottley (1914), p. 299.

[3] H. St J. Thackeray, *The Septuagint and Jewish Worship* (1921), p. 13; S. Jellicoe, *The Septuagint and Modern Study* (1968), p. 317.

Holy art thou, who art stronger than every power.
Holy art thou, who art greater than all excellence.
Holy art thou, who art better than praises.

This is not Semitic, and it is not verse; it is a prose hymn, whose short lines are determined by reasons of content rather than form.

With this I return to the Prologue. It is impossible to draw the kind of dividing line that might enable the reader to assign some verses to a source written in poetry, and others to a prose-writing evangelist. We may ask whether there are breaks in sense, which would lead us to suspect the activity of a more or less unintelligent editor; but this is a matter of exegesis. And we may inquire why in some passages the evangelist was moved to more lyrical expression than in others. The reason for this is not hard to find; and it leads me to the next point of development in this study.

A little while ago I referred to the considerable measure of disagreement manifested by the eight authors whose analyses of the Prologue are tabulated by R. E. Brown. All eight, however, are agreed in omitting verses 6–8, 15, which deal with the witness of the Baptist. These verses, says one author after another, are prose insertions in a poetical Prologue. But if I am right, this is an impossible distinction. In fact, these verses are more rhythmical than is often allowed, and can be set out in parallel couplets:

> There came a man, sent from God,
> His name was John.
> He came to bear witness of the light,
> That through him all men might believe.
> This John (ἐκεῖνος) was not the light;
> He came to bear witness of the light.

If they are less rhythmical than the rest, it is because they stand closer to the old tradition. This is especially true of verse 15. With these observations in mind, and in the hope of throwing some fresh light on a disputed subject, I propose to begin with these references to John the Baptist. It has been almost universally supposed that they are interpolations, not belonging to the original form of the Prologue. Let us see how we fare if, instead of treating them as later supplements, looked at last of all (if looked at at all), we begin with them.

It is often said that John's handling of the traditional material about the Baptist was influenced by his desire to refute the beliefs of a Baptist sect, which made higher claims for their master than an orthodox Christian could accept. John, the sect alleged, was the Messiah; the Gospel makes him affirm that he is not (1.20). Some who believe that the present Johannine Prologue was founded upon an earlier hymn believe that hymn to have originated in the Baptist sect, so that its present form represents an appropriation by a Christian of a hymn to John the Baptist as the Logos, in which verses 6–8(9),15 were inserted in order to make it clear that the Baptist was now to be regarded not as the central but as a strictly subordinate figure. There may well be truth in the view that the evangelist had among his interests that of combating a Baptist group. It is true that the evidence for the existence of such a group is not quite so definite as has been thought;[1] Käsemann, for example, is probably right in seeing theological and ecclesiastical rather than simply historical motivation behind the reference in Acts 19.1–7 to a group of disciples in Ephesus who are said to have received only John's baptism, and to know nothing of the gift of the Spirit. Nevertheless, evidence for a persisting group of disciples of John does exist, and it is quite reasonable to suppose that John the Evangelist disagreed with them, and took the opportunity of writing a Gospel to say so, though of course this in itself does not require a literary theory of prose interpolations into a primitive Prologue. This is, I say, a reasonable view, but it is scarcely adequate to explain what the evangelist says. For example, it does not explain why the evangelist makes John deny not only that he is the Messiah but also that he is Elijah (1.21), an identification made in the earlier tradition—in so many words in Matthew (17.13), and by very clear implication in Mark (9.13) and Luke (1.17). Nor does it explain why the evangelist lays so much stress on the testimony of John, who not only repeats the synoptic saying about the One who comes after him (1.27, 30), but also bears witness to Jesus as the Lamb of God (1.29, 36), and as the one who baptizes with the Holy Spirit (1.33), and is as much superior to the Baptist as the bridegroom to the groomsman (3.29).

We should at this stage recall that if there existed a Baptist sect, which (from the Christian point of view) overrated John, there was

---

[1] I may refer here to an unpublished Durham thesis (*Disciples of John the Baptist: an examination of the evidence of their existence, and an estimate of their significance for the study of the Fourth Gospel*) by J. H. Hughes.

also in the second century an opposite tendency. The anti-Baptist movement has far stronger historical attestation, and must have been more numerous, than the pro-Baptist. Marcion was one of its leaders. He appears to have taken Luke 7.23 (Blessed is he who is not offended in me) to mean that John the Baptist was offended by Jesus: Tertullian writes,[1] John is offended when he hears of the miracles of Christ, as if they were those of a strange god (*Scandalizatur Johannes auditis virtutibus Christi ut alterius*). Anti-Marcionite writers insist, against both the literary and the theological criticism of Marcion, that John the Baptist belongs to the beginning of the gospel (and incidentally to its completion too). The anti-Marcionite prologue to Luke includes the words: "We have received therefore as most essential, right at the beginning, the birth of John, who is the beginning of the gospel. He was the Lord's forerunner and partner both in the perfection of the gospel and in the experience of baptism and in the fellowship of the Spirit." The Muratorian Canon reflects the same concern, though less emphatically: "[Luke] begins to write from the birth of John." Evidently in the latter half of the second century orthodox writers over against Marcion had to insist on John the Baptist's place in the gospel, a place that was typified for them by his appearance "in the beginning" of Luke's Gospel—the record of his conception and birth interlocking with that of Jesus, his ministry immediately preceding and linked, through baptism and the Spirit, with that of Jesus.

The Fourth Evangelist has been seen by some as standing on, though not far along, the same road as Marcion. Harnack, in a passage that strikingly anticipates Käsemann's "Johanning docetism", writes:

> In the conversation of Jesus with the Samaritan woman, John, going far beyond Paul, sets both Jewish and heathen worship over against the new worship in Spirit and in truth as essentially similar and equally false; like Marcion, he can make Jesus say that all that came before him were robbers and murderers; like Marcion, he excludes the proclamation of grace and truth from the Old Testament—all Moses proclaimed was the law. But further: we are on the road to Marcion when John (although Matthew and Luke had already written their Gospels) considers it superfluous to speak of the birth of Christ, when he

[1] *Adv. Marcionem* 4. 18.

D

moreover depresses the significance of the baptism of Christ to a sign which is supposed to have been given to the Baptist, and when, though he does indeed proclaim the message, "The Word became flesh", he yet treats the human element in Christ as a shadowy apparition.[1]

Cullmann sets the evangelist on a somewhat different line of development:

> Only the *Preaching of Peter*, which has preserved the gnostic ideas in their purest form, and, in this respect, is even more closely connected with baptism than the Gospel of John, takes the final step. It attacks the person of John the Baptist himself. While in the Synoptic Gospels John is still a prophet, and in the Fourth Gospel this title is refused him, in the *Preaching of Peter* he becomes a false prophet.[2]

Both Harnack and Cullmann have, I think, drawn attention to interesting phenomena, and have placed the Fourth Evangelist's handling of John the Baptist in illuminating contexts; they have not, however, got the picture in true perspective and focus. It is true that in the Fourth Gospel John denies that he is the Christ; but no Christian ever believed that he was, since by definition the Christian knew that the role of Messiah was filled by Jesus and no other. Here John the Evangelist stands on precisely the same ground as Matthew, Mark, and Luke; there is no progressive denigration of the Baptist in this. It is also true that in the Fourth Gospel John is made to deny that he is Elijah, and here this Gospel is in contradiction with the others. This, however, is not to say that the figure of the Baptist is being lowered in estimation; it may be that the evangelist's intention is the reverse of this. When the Baptist denies that he is Elijah (1.21) he goes on to claim (1.23), in the words of Isaiah 40.3, that he is "the voice of one crying in the wilderness, Make straight the way of the Lord". This comes near to saying that the Baptist is himself the voice of the Old Testament, the witness to salvation (4.22; cf. 5.46), the agency responsible for making the unique coming of the Lord intelligible (cf. 1.7, "That through him all men might believe"). The parallel between John the Baptist and the Old Testament is closest in 5.35, 39 (especially if

---

[1] *Marcion: das Evangelium vom fremden Gott* (Leipzig 1921), p. 238.

[2] *Le Problème littéraire et historique du Roman Pseudo-Clémentin* (Paris 1930), p. 240.

A. T. Hanson[1] is right in thinking that the imagery of 5.35 is based on Psalm 132, and that John is being described, in terms of that Psalm, as a "lamp for my anointed", a witness to the true light). The Jews drew religious delight from John's ministry, as they also enjoyed searching the Scriptures; yet they would not pay attention to him to whom both John and the Scriptures pointed them.

To depict John the Baptist as a summary, a crystallization of the Old Testament, and, if we may follow Hanson so far, of the Jewish cultus too, is certainly not to yield to the claims of a Baptist sect which regarded John as himself the Messiah, the true light; yet at the same time it yields to neither Marcionite nor Jewish Christian denigration of John, but rather maintains the synoptic position that outside the kingdom of God, apart, that is, from all that came into the world in and through Jesus, there is none greater than John, but that anything that falls within the area of fulfilment is necessarily greater than that which is being fulfilled (Matt. 11.11; Luke 7.28). Having gone so far we can take a further step. The Old Testament, and still more clearly the Jews, stand in a curiously ambiguous position in the Fourth Gospel. On the one hand, the Scripture cannot be broken (10.35), and salvation is of the Jews (4.22). Yet the Jews are the enemies of Jesus, and they have made of their law one that decrees that he ought to die (19.7). This, in the evangelist's view, is what happens when the people of God choose to regard themselves and their sacred writings as complete in themselves, so that, in their own estimation, they are free, they have light and can see, they have life. When this happens, it is not the fault of the Old Testament; it is the fault of those who misuse it. In the same way, if John the Baptist is regarded as himself the true and primary light, the fault is not his. When not misused, the Old Testament and John have positive and abiding value; yet, despite themselves, they can be, have been, and are misused, and it is therefore necessary to fence them about with some strict negatives.

This happens in the course of the Gospel—every time, perhaps, that John is mentioned. In chapter 1 he denies that he is the Christ, Elijah, or the prophet, and affirms his unworthiness over against the Coming One; in chapter 3 he describes himself as the groomsman, not the bridegroom; in chapter 4 he makes and baptizes fewer disciples than Jesus; in chapter 5 he is the secondary,

[1] *Studies in the Pastoral Epistles* (1968), pp. 12ff.

derivative light. It happens also in the Prologue, to which, with this observation, we may return.

What the Prologue says about John the Baptist is a summary of the extended narrative treatment in chapters 1, 3, 4. In 1.15 later material is actually quoted in an awkward manner which evidently presupposes that the reader of the Prologue must be familiar with the narrative that follows: "This is he of whom I said, He who comes after me has come to be before me, for he was before me." John bears witness, he points away from himself, he points to Christ. This, however, is done, in the Prologue, not in narrative but in theological terms. The narrative is indeed presupposed, and the words of the Prologue would—even in verses 6–8—make little sense to one who did not know it; but the Prologue itself contains (to borrow a phrase) only the "that" and not the "what" or the "how" of the historical narrative. There appeared on the plane of history a man sent from God; his name was John. This is history, but it is also part of the theology, for that God sends a man, a unique, particular man, who has a name, into the world is a theological before it is an historical proposition. It means that God, who, with his Logos, is eternally what he is, and is beyond definition, enters the world of time and space (and definition); first through a messenger, but secondly also in his own person. After this opening, which asserts the action of God in time, the language is entirely theological: witness, light, believe. The words of verse 15 may be intended to convey the hint that Jesus before his public ministry had once been a follower of John, but they are so chosen as to express the subsequent emergence in time of one whose being spanned eternity before and after John. Briefly, what the Prologue contains (in the verses to which we are at present confining our attention) is a theological evaluation of the historical figure of the Baptist; it places the narrative that is to follow in the setting in which it can be understood. This means that the "Baptist" verses were not an afterthought, thrown in to injure the rival Baptist group, but part of a serious, connected, thought-out, theological purpose. I repeat: there is good, though not overwhelming, reason to think that such a Baptist group did form part of the environment within which John wrote, just as "the Jews", as he comprehensively termed them, formed another part. But as John takes and uses as an instrument of his theological evaluation of Jesus the paradoxical twofold relationship, of filiation and opposition, between Christians and Jews, so he employs in the same overall theological task the similar relationship between the Baptist and Jesus. John was not engaging in a pamphlet war, either with Judaism or with the disciples of John the Baptist, but writing theology in a book that was to be a possession for ever. In this theology, both the Jews and their book, and John the Baptist, had essential parts to play as witnesses to the central character, true and valid precisely so long as they were not overvalued, and confused with that to which their testimony was directed.

If this is the origin and the meaning of the "Baptist" verses in the Prologue, it is reasonable to suppose that this will also be the origin and meaning of the rest; that is, that, as these verses were designed to bring out the theological significance of the story of the Baptist, so the Prologue as a whole was designed to bring out the theological significance of the history of Jesus; in fact, however, this theology is necessarily set out in what may be called not merely an historical but a chronological framework. Thus the Prologue cannot begin with John the Baptist. The evangelist knows that however indispensable the figure of the Baptist may be (and he by no means dispenses with him) he is not the *beginning* of the gospel. Mark and Luke may have said this, and the Anti-Marcionite Prologue writer underlined it, but they exaggerated, for the true *beginning* lies not merely at (as Gen. 1.1 suggests) but before the creation, before time itself. There and then (if in such a setting the words are meaningful) God's self-disclosure was implicit in the being of God himself. "In the beginning was the Word, and the Word was with God, and the Word was God." God was never without self-expression (*logos*), and the self-expression was itself God. God in revelation is God in himself, not a secondary form of deity. Hence creation, the first form of divine self-expression: "All things came into being through him, and apart from him there came into being not one thing that has come into being." Hence, further, life and light, the primary forms in which self-expression in creation becomes communicable; and if you say light, you must be prepared to say darkness too, though not a darkness that stands on equal terms with the light. "The light shines [simply because it is light—we are not yet, in verse 5, dealing with the incarnation] in the darkness, and the darkness has never quenched it." All this occupies the first five verses, which describe the stage on which men must live, and God means to intervene. They do not yet describe the historical coming of the Word into the world, but state the factors—God, Word, light, life, darkness—that will be involved in his coming. We are, however, ready for history, and immediately it comes, though it is not the coming of the Word, the history of Jesus. "There was a man sent from God—his name, John." His appearance was a divine act, but it was not the coming of the true light, who is the Logos, who is God. It was the indispensable testimony to this coming, without which men could not understand what was happening, and therefore could not believe. The mission of John was that men might believe not in but through him, and it is after but in immediate connection with his coming that the coming of the Word takes place. Even so, when the true light shone in the person of Jesus (cf. 8.12; 9.5; 12.35, 46), men did not believe; he came to his home, and his own people did not receive him. This, however, is not a universal negative; there were those who did receive him, and to them he gave the power to become children of God, by supernatural birth. This exception (verse 12) to the rejection is not an interpolated afterthought, but is necessary if the evangelist is not to cut his own throat; no Church (unless perhaps in the twentieth century) ever sang a hymn to celebrate its own unbelief. Verse 13 is not a gloss, but an allusion to the Virgin Birth; the Prologue reaches its climax in the assertion that Christians share the miraculous origin of their Lord.

This takes us up to verse 13, and gives a complete theological account of the pre-existence of the Word and the work of the Baptist, of the coming of the Word and the ministry of Jesus, which resulted in the supernatural birth of the children of God. One might well ask why, after this climax, the Prologue continues, and though, for reasons some of which I have given, I cannot accept Käsemann's view that the original form of the Prologue came to an end at verse 12, it is his great service that he has brought this question into relief. So far from being the climax of the Prologue, verse 14 ("The Word became flesh") appears at first sight to be a mere appendage. Käsemann sets the question in terms of source criticism, and gives a corresponding answer: verses 14–18 are a supplement to the original Prologue; in view of the fact that our analysis of the Prologue began from John the Baptist we may put the question in the form, "Why does John divide his Baptist material into two parts? That is, why is verse 15 separated from verses 6–8(9)?" To put the question thus with reference to John the Baptist will enable us to answer the total problem with reference to verses 14–18 as a whole.

The two passages, verses 6–8 and 15, must serve different purposes. The earlier reference to the Baptist (verses 6–8) provides his witness to the pre-existent light and its coming into the world; verse 15 ("John bears witness of him, and cried, saying: 'This is he of whom I spoke; he who comes after me has taken his place in front of me, for he was before me'") refers primarily not (as Bernard said) to the pre-existence of the Word, which John has already dealt with, but to his glorification. True, this rests upon his pre-existence: "For he was before me" (cf. 17.5); but what is said in this verse is that he who first appeared as a successor, perhaps as a follower, of the Baptist has now taken rank in front of him. This gives us the clue that we need. Of the Prologue, verses 1–13 have told us in theological terms how the pre-existent Logos or light came to the world that he had created, and was rejected in it, though rejected in such a way that those who did receive him found in the rejected one their own true life, and regeneration as the children of God. But this is not the end of the story. Rejection is not the last word, nor even is regeneration. The humble follower of John was exalted to a position of pre-eminence beyond the greatest of men. This is the old tradition—the story of the resurrection and *parousia* of the Son of man, the exaltation to lordship of the humble servant who was obedient even unto death. The evangelist, however (as we well know, having read the rest of the Gospel), has more to say than this. Humble, sacrificial love *is* glory, and there is none more exalted. Hence the next stage in the Prologue.

"The Word became flesh"—Käsemann is right; this is not where the stress lies. It merely resumes what has been said in verses 9–11, but it resumes it in the most paradoxical terms possible—and in this Bultmann is right too. The manifestation of which we are to hear in a moment was not automatic, nor was it assessable by ordinary measures; it was accessible only to faith. But John continues: "He dwelt among us, and we beheld his glory." This is the point. When did we behold his glory? Not at the last day, for John uses the past tense, We beheld; it was in the ministry, the loving service and sacrifice of Jesus, that we beheld his glory. For what is glory? It is to be "full of grace and truth". The exaltation the Baptist predicted has taken place, in the fruit of

Jesus' work, "for of his fullness we have all received, grace upon grace". And what is grace? John can define it only as Paul defined it, in contrast with law. "The law was given through Moses; grace and truth came through Jesus Christ." But grace is matched with truth, and the coming of grace and truth *is* the revelation of God. So the wheel turns full circle, and the Prologue ends where it began, with the revelation of God implicit in the being of God himself—"the Only-begotten, who is in the bosom of the Father". God himself is self-disclosing, self-imparting love, and the revelation is the glory of love, which is light and life.

The Prologue is not a jig-saw puzzle but one piece of solid theological writing. The evangelist wrote it all, recalling as he did so who knows what pieces of wisdom and logos speculation, and it sums up the meaning he had seen in the story of Jesus. If the relation of Prologue to Gospel is to be summed up in a word I should take up again language I used specifically of the place in it of John the Baptist. It is even more apt to the place of Jesus, the Word. Prologue and Gospel together are the supreme example of the coinherence of the "that" and the "what" of the story of Jesus. The Prologue assumes simply that the light shone in the darkness, that he came to his own, that the Word became flesh, and analyses the theological significance of the bare fact expressed in the "that". The Gospel will tell how he came to his own, what happened when the Word became flesh. And the Prologue is necessary to the Gospel, as the Gospel is necessary to the Prologue. The history explicates the theology, and the theology interprets the history.

4

The Dialectical Theology of St John

It might seem reasonable to begin a study of this subject with a definition of the phrase "dialectical theology". Such a definition I do not propose to offer, for several reasons. Of these not the least is that I am far from sure that I know what "dialectical theology" means when the term is not used in a context that defines it. It is, I suspect, one of those useful phrases whose virtue—or, if you prefer it, defect—is that they can be used in a variety of ways according to the user's taste; and, in the familiar words that Papias applied to a different matter, each man interprets them as he is able. This perhaps too flippant observation does not mean that I have learned nothing from the dialectical theology of our own age: it means that my main reason for offering no definitions at the outset of this study is that I believe that it will be better to let the meaning of "the dialectical theology of St John" appear naturally, as I think it will, at the end of our investigation than to anticipate it at the beginning.

I must, however, linger for a moment on the word "dialectical". How far the Kantian delineation of contradictory principles, and the Hegelian reconciliation of such principles in a higher comprehensive truth, may be said to have their roots in the original Socratic τεχνή διαλεκτική is too wide a question for a preliminary note. For myself I suspect that the roots are to be found if not in the Socratic theory at least in the Socratic practice. In Socratic dialogue—and dialogue (διαλέγεσθαι) is dialectic—concepts are looked at first from one side then from another, definitions are proposed, attacked, defended, abandoned, or improved, opposite points of view are canvassed and, sometimes at least, combined. And the process of thought itself is conceived as fundamentally unspoken dialogue.

SOCRATES. Do you mean by thinking the same which I mean?

THEAETUS. What is that?

SOCRATES. I mean the conversation which the soul holds with herself in considering of anything. I speak of what I scarcely know; but the soul when thinking (διανοουμένη) appears to me to be just talking (οὐκ ἄλλο τι ἢ διαλέγεσθαι)—asking questions of herself and answering them, affirming and denying (φάσκουσα καὶ οὐ φάσκουσα). And when she has arrived at a decision, either gradually or by a sudden impulse, and has at last agreed, and does not doubt, this is called her opinion (δόξαν). I say, then, that to form an opinion is to speak, and opinion is a word spoken, I mean, to oneself and in silence, not aloud or to another.[1]

Thus, a dialectical system of thought, whether specifically theological or more generally philosophical, is one whose method is debate. The debate may be conducted externally between a number of persons, as in a Socratic dialogue, or internally, when the solitary thinker himself evolves propositions and counter-propositions for inward disputation. When thinking of this kind takes place, the result may be the triumph of one view over another, the reconciling of two views in a higher unity, or the simple retention of two not immediately reconcilable opinions in an uneasy paradox. Of the last kind of result the classical Christian example is the Chalcedonian Definition, where the Fathers properly and successfully insisted upon the two natures, divine and human, but were much less successful in showing how the two natures could be united in one real person.

Here, however, we have as much definition as we need. I have no intention of going on to define "dialectical theology" and then turning the pages of the Fourth Gospel to see if I can find what I have defined. We shall begin with the text, and see what it has to offer us. And here I must at once proceed to some fairly drastic delimitation. I have spoken of the "dialectical theology of St John". For the purpose of this study "St John" means the author of the Fourth Gospel; nothing is implied with regard to the authorship of the Epistles and Revelation, but they will appear marginally at most. The Fourth Gospel, moreover, is itself a fairly substantial work, and though I shall glance at other parts of it I shall concentrate on chapter 6.

[1] Plato, *Theaetetus* 189E, 190A (Jowett's translation).

There are, I think, good reasons for doing this. In several respects this chapter stands at the centre of current Johannine debate. This is true in regard to both critical and theological questions. The former will lead us to the latter. Perhaps the most widely accepted transposition of material in the Gospel is that which reverses the order of chapters 5 and 6. On this let me simply observe that it raises immediately a fundamental question with regard to the purpose and interpretation of the book. To reverse the order of these chapters undoubtedly provides a smoother itinerary; at the same time it disturbs what seems to be a carefully thought out theological sequence, in which the first of the great christological "I am" claims (6.35) is preceded, and thus interpreted, by the most outspoken assertion of the Son's unqualified obedience to, and dependence on, the Father (5.19–23). Which is decisive for John—topography or theology? This is not as simple a question as may appear when stated rhetorically like this; it is possible that the basic Johannine source was topographically sound, and was rearranged in the interests of theology.

This observation leads to a further critical question, that of sources. Chapter 6 contains more contacts with the Synoptic Gospels than do most chapters in the Fourth Gospel. These are: the miraculous feeding, the walking of Jesus on the lake, his teaching at Capernaum, the use of material that recalls the Last Supper sayings about loaf and cup, and a confession of faith by Simon Peter. Is all this a Johannine rewriting of Mark? use not of Mark but of something more loosely definable as "synoptic tradition"? or tradition parallel but distinct? Again, the critical question, if we can answer it, will help to provide material for theological evaluation. There is a further question in the realm of source criticism. Chapter 6 contains two miracle stories, the feeding of the five thousand and the walking on the lake; it also contains a long and characteristically Johannine discourse on the Bread of Life. How are sign and discourse related? Are we to assign them to two distinct sources, a σημεῖα-Quelle and the Offenbarungsreden? If so, what were the origins and original characteristics of these sources, and how did they come to be combined? If not, was the discourse constructed to fit the signs?

Finally, it may be asked whether we have this chapter in the form in which it left the author's hand. Chapter 6 is one of those parts of the Gospel where the theory of ecclesiastical redaction and interpolation is most important, and the questions raised by it are most acute. It has been held that unevenness of literary composition combines with inconsistency of thought to disclose the work of an editor, and that it is possible to remove the redactional supplements, restore the order, and thus establish the original form of the Gospel, a form in which it was at variance with received doctrine. This critical problem I am stating here in the most general terms, partly because I shall return to it, and partly because merely to state it provides me with a bridge to the theological questions raised by the chapter. Of these I shall mention at this stage only two, but these are the most familiar and perhaps the most important.

The chapter contains some of the clearest statements of "realized" or "present" eschatology to be found anywhere in the New Testament.

He who believes has ($\check{\epsilon}\chi\epsilon\iota$) eternal life (6.47).

This is the bread that comes down out of heaven, that one should eat of it and not die. I am the living bread that came down out of heaven; if anyone eats of this bread he shall live for ever (6.50f).

He who eats this bread shall live for ever (6.58).

These passages seem clear. Eternal life is offered and possessed here and now; and the possessor, the man who is related to God in Christ, will not die but will live for ever. Over against these verses, however, there stands a sequence in which, in slightly varying words, it is promised that the believer will be raised up at the last day (6.39, 40, 44, 54). But how can he be raised up if he never dies, and already possesses eternal life?

The second theological question follows at once. Granted that the believer, in some sense which may still await definition, possesses eternal life, how does he receive it? One answer provided by the chapter is that he receives it simply as a believer, that is, as one who is drawn to Jesus, hears and believes his word, and abides in him.

This is the work God requires, that you believe in him whom he sent (6.29).

He who comes to me shall never hunger, and he who believes in me shall never thirst (6.35).

This is the will of my Father, that everyone who beholds the Son and believes in him should have eternal life (6.40).

He who believes has eternal life (6.47).

It is the Spirit that gives life; the flesh is no use at all; the words that I have spoken to you are Spirit and are life (6.63).

Over against these verses, however, is to be set a passage (6.53–8) which has very commonly been interpreted with reference to the Eucharist, and naturally so, since it refers not only to eating the flesh but also to drinking the blood of the Son of man.

Unless you eat the flesh of the Son of man and drink his blood, you have no life in yourselves. He who eats my flesh and drinks my blood has eternal life, and I will raise him up at the last day. For my flesh is truly food and my blood is truly drink (6.53ff).

Does John then teach that communion with the Son, and the gift of eternal life, are exclusively dependent on sacramental means (53)? or that such physical media ($\sigma \acute{\alpha} \rho \xi$) are worthless (63)?

I have already mentioned the theory of ecclesiastical redaction, and the reader will be aware of the view, argued most impressively by Dr R. Bultmann, that in its original form the Johannine material taught a purely spiritual relation of the believer to Christ which conveyed the gift of eternal life in the present, an eternal life which already carried with it and conferred inward victory over death, and that this Johannine theology was brought into line with Christian belief at the end of the first century by the interpolation of references to the crude futurist eschatology of a resurrection at the last day, and of a passage which alluded to the Eucharist in terms reminiscent of Ignatius' sacramentalism: the flesh and blood, the bread and wine, were a $\phi \acute{\alpha} \rho \mu \alpha \kappa o \nu$ $\dot{\alpha} \theta \alpha \nu \alpha \sigma \acute{\iota} \alpha \varsigma$, a medicine of immortality, indispensably necessary to the possession of eternal life, and automatically effecting it.

It was my intention when I embarked upon this study to introduce at this point not the bare reference to Dr Bultmann that I have just given, but a much fuller account of those who have attacked the literary and theological unity of this chapter, and of those who have defended it. It has now become clear to me that this would be a bibliographical luxury which I cannot allow myself —possibly a bibliographical boredom which I may well spare my readers. Those who wish for further references may find them in, for example, R. E. Brown's excellent commentary, and in D. M. Smith's *The Composition and Order of the Fourth Gospel*. That this chapter has proved to be a centre of debate is not accidental, but bears witness to the fact that it is one of the key-points in the development of Johannine theology. This fact is evident enough. John 6 sets forth Jesus as the transcendent fulfilment of the Old Testament, who attracts to himself as a personal predicate the first of a number of fundamental images—I am the bread of life (35), stands in a unique relation to God the Father (27) and accomplishes his will (38), and is confessed by the representative disciple, Peter, as the Holy One of God (69). It is crucial to the understanding of the Gospel as a whole that we should know whether this chapter is a unity with a coherent and distinctive message, or whether its primary theme has been obscured or even contradicted by a patchwork of glosses and interpolations.

Before we tackle this question in such detail as our time permits, let me make one general observation. There are undoubtedly themes in regard to which the Gospel presents a double front, and refuses to allow its readers to adopt a simple, uncomplicated attitude. Some of these themes I have recently discussed elsewhere,[1] and may mention here only briefly. They are indeed familiar enough. For example, the relation of the Gospel to Judaism is complex. There is said to be a Semitic element in John's Greek style; there are signs of familiarity with Jewish customs and Jewish exegesis; there is perhaps evidence of acquaintance with the Judean countryside. This Jewishness may be summed up, and taken further, in the proposition (4.22), "Salvation is of the Jews"; salvation, that is, is the fulfilment of that which God promised in the Old Testament to the Jewish race, and it must be worked out in the midst of the Jewish people, and in terms of Jewish religious institutions and theological conceptions. Yet, if salvation is of the Jews, it may also be asserted that the Jews are sprung from their father the devil (8.44). They are the implacable enemies of Jesus, in whom the event of salvation takes place, and make of their God-given law an instrument for securing his death (19.7). The Gospel is both Jewish and anti-Jewish, and this antinomy is due neither to negligence in the handling of inconsistent sources, nor to the insertion by means of contradictory

---

[1] *Das Johannesevangelium und das Judentum* (Stuttgart 1970).

glosses of a new viewpoint into a book whose position had already been made clear. It arises out of John's understanding of the theological—the theological rather than the sociological—setting of Christianity, and this may be traced back certainly to the earliest Christian tradition, and with a high measure of probability to Jesus himself; for if any two propositions about the historical Jesus can be asserted with confidence, they are that he was a Jew, and that he was rejected by his fellow-Jews. Christianity and Judaism stand side by side, linked uneasily by a unique similarity and a unique dissimilarity to which John has given pointed expression.

It is equally true, and would I think be fairly widely agreed, that John is both gnostic and anti-gnostic. The gnostic background of thought and language which is characteristic of the Gospel as a whole, and the anti-gnostic twist given to this thought and language, are both illustrated in the concluding verses of the prayer in chapter 17:

> Righteous Father, the world did not know thee, but I knew thee, and these men knew that thou didst send me; and I have made known to them thy name, and will make it known, that the love with which thou didst love me may be in them, and I in them (17.25f).

Here are the familiar themes of the ignorant world, and of the revealer who alone knows the true God and is sent by him to communicate the truth to the elect; but the purpose of this sending is the cultivation not of gnosis but of love, which alone is the mark of true disciples (13.35). Here too we have an antinomy that is written into the stuff of the Gospel, and can be so written because the themes of gnosticism are up to a point true, and even its mythological language—the use of the pair, light and darkness, for example—had already been employed in early Christian tradition, since they belonged equally to the language of apocalyptic.

These observations mean that, when we turn to the particular problems of chapter 6, we shall at any rate not leap to the conclusion that the expression of differing points of view must needs betray the hand of an interpolator, inserting his own thoughts into an existing text without regard for consistency and continuity, but consider rather that the author may have elected to express his theme in dialectical fashion, looking at it now from this side, now from that. Indeed, it is possible that it was not so much the author who imposed this form upon his material, as the material that imposed the form upon him. Before, however, we can state this kind of conclusion we have important steps to take.

First, there are considerations of a literary and critical kind, which, though we cannot discuss them in detail, it would be wrong wholly to ignore.

1. The chapter should be examined from the point of view of Johannine characteristics and vocabulary. To do this in detail is manifestly impossible, nor is it necessary. The crucial passage (6.51–8) has been repeatedly studied in this way, and the facts are hardly in doubt. It contains both Johannine and unjohannine features. This has been briefly but clearly brought out by Eduard Schweizer,[1] who notes on the one hand οὖν *historicum*, the construction καθὼς . . . καὶ. . ., "on the last day", the doubled ἀμήν, and ἐὰν μή. . . οὐ . . .; and on the other φαγεῖν and πίνειν with the accusative instead of ἐκ, ἐξ οὐρανοῦ (instead of ἐκ τοῦ οὐρανοῦ), οἱ πατέρες (without ἡμῶν or ὑμῶν), and ἀληθής instead of ἀληθινός. Dr Schweizer thinks the evidence too evenly balanced for a literary judgement; perhaps he is right, but he himself does something to weaken the force of the unjohannine characteristics, and more could be done—for example, if instead of ἀληθής we read (with (א*) (D) Θ ℜ lat sy) ἀληθῶς, which may well be original and would not be unjohannine (cf. 1.47; 4.42; 6.14; 7.26, 40; 8.31; 17.8). Only the meaning of verses 51–8, and their relation, or lack of relation, with the context, can justify the removal of these verses as a redactional gloss.

The same may be said of the phrase ἀναστήσω αὐτὸ(ν) (ἐν) τῇ ἐσχάτῃ ἡμέρᾳ, which occurs four times. In verse 54 it falls within the longer passage, 51–8, which we have just considered. This Dr Bultmann regards as the source of the other three occurrences. It raises no problem for him here, since the whole passage is on his view part of the ecclesiastical redaction. It is worth noting that the redactor at least found no difficulty in combining present and future: "He who eats has eternal life, and I will raise him up at the last day." The words occur also in verses 39, 40, 44. Even without the excellent rabbinic parallel (Exod. R. 38.3) cited by P. Borgen,[2] verses 39, 40 give rise to no difficulty. In each case

[1] "Das johanneische Zeugnis vom Herrenmahl", *Evangelische Theologie* 8 (1952–3), pp. 341–63.
[2] P. Borgen, *Bread from Heaven* (Leiden 1965), pp. 77f.

ἀναστήσω is dependent on the same ἵνα as the preceding clause:

39: This is the will of him who sent me, namely, that I should not lose . . ., but should raise up . . .

40: This is the will of my Father, namely, that he who beholds and believes should have . . ., and that I should raise . . .

Verse 44 is more difficult, and the conditional construction means that Dr Borgen's parallel is less effective. It is possible but awkward to take ἀναστήσω as a subjunctive parallel with ἑλκύσῃ: . . . unless the Father draws . . . and I raise up. It seems, however, more probable that here ἀναστήσω is a future indicative, and constitutes a new sentence.

44: No one can come to me, unless the Father who sent me draws him. And I for my part (κἀγώ) will raise him up at the last day.

Such a complete additional sentence could have been added by a redactor, dissatisfied with the text and wishing to introduce a new idea. This however does not necessarily mean that it was so added, since an author is always at liberty to put a new thought in a new sentence. It is clear that once more we are dealing with an issue that can be settled only on exegetical and theological grounds; and this is as true of the references to a future resurrection in verses 39 and 40 as of that in 44.

2. It is much harder in little space to summarize and discuss Dr Bultmann's view of the disruption which he believes to have taken place in the remainder of the chapter, which he takes to have stood originally in the order 27, 34, 35, 30–3, 47–51a, 41–6, 36–40, 59. Such wholesale rearrangement clearly turns upon exegesis. I cannot here embark upon verse by verse exegesis, but I should like to draw attention to the work that has been done, especially by Dr Peder Borgen, on the exegetical background of John 6. It is clear to any reader that the discourse on the Bread of Life reflects the Old Testament story of the provision of Manna (Exod. 16), and the comment on this in Psalm 78.24, "He gave them bread from heaven to eat". It seems, however, possible to go a good deal further than this. Dr Borgen summarizes his main conclusion as follows:

E

In this exposition [i.e., of the pericope on the manna], both Philo (Mut. 258–260, Leg. all. III 162, 168 and Congr. 170, 173–174) and John (6.31–58) paraphrased words from the Old Testament quotations and interwove them with fragments from the Haggadah about manna. The main haggadic traditions upon which Philo drew can be identified with certainty; those upon which John is dependent with a great degree of probability.[1]

This is not the place to expound, still less to discuss, Dr Borgen's views in detail. Some may think that he uses, in the passage I have just cited, the words "certainty", "probability", rather more confidently than they would. But if his conclusions are at all valid, they mean that the dislocation and redaction theory is not the only means of explaining the material in this chapter, and the case for examining the chapter as it stands, with the intention of finding out what it says on the main themes it contains, is correspondingly strengthened. This examination is our main task.

1. The chapter begins with a general reference to the σημεῖα which Jesus performed (2). In this verse the signs are miracles of healing, and they are said to have attracted the presence of a large crowd, who saw them (ἐώρων). Jesus, who has gone up into a mountain, sees the crowd, and the story of the feeding of the five thousand is set in motion. We have no time to linger over its details (though some of them are important). The whole multitude has enough and to spare. In verse 14 this event is described as a σημεῖον, and those who saw it are moved to draw the conclusion, "Truly this man is the prophet who is due to come (ὁ ἐρχόμενος) into the world". Jesus is thus identified with the messianic prophet of the last days, and in the next verse we learn that the people intend to make him king. Upon this follows the appearance of Jesus to his disciples as they cross the lake. I question whether Dr Borgen is right in describing this as a theophanic appearance,[2] but it certainly underlines the supernatural authority of Jesus (25). It is upon this that Jesus declares to the crowds who have followed him to Capernaum:

Truly, truly I tell you, you are seeking me not because you saw (εἴδετε) signs (σημεῖα), but because you ate some of the loaves and were satisfied (verse 26).

---

[1] Op. cit., p. 1.   [2] Op. cit., e.g. p. 180.

The word "sign" occurs once more, in the challenge of the crowd:

What sign then are you doing, that we may see (it) and believe you? (verse 30).

It has been well observed that these references to "signs" do not fit neatly together. First, we learn that the crowd saw signs and were deeply impressed by them. Next, the feeding is described as a sign, and those who witness it are moved to at least a partial apprehension of the truth about Jesus: they perceive that he is a messianic figure (which John himself believed), holding him to be the prophet and wishing to make him king. Next, however, Jesus declares that the crowds are interested only in free meals; it is implied that though they had enjoyed the food they had not truly witnessed signs; the οὐχ ὅτι εἴδετε of verse 26 contradicts the ἑώρων of verse 2. The negative view recurs in verse 30, where the request for a sign implies that those who make it have not recognized that what has just been done in their presence is a sign, and one greater than any that Moses could claim. It is not an adequate explanation to say that the crowds had witnessed the signs without perceiving that they were signs, that is, without perceiving the truth signified by such outward acts as the supplying of hungry people with food. This is true as far as it goes, but it does not account for the negative parallelism of verse 2 and verse 26: they saw (ἑώρων) and they did not see (οὐκ εἴδετε) signs. Again it is a correct but superficial observation that the word "sign" changes, or rather deepens, its meaning. In verse 2 σημεῖα ἐπὶ τῶν ἀσθενούντων are, as the participial clause shows, "healing miracles". In verse 26 (and 30) signs are manifestations of divine truth. The dialectical movement of John's thought as he wrestles with the question, What is a sign? is clear. But there is more to say than this. The crowds saw, and they did not see, signs. They believed in Jesus, yet they did not believe in him. The meaning of seeing and of believing, two vital and related themes for the Gospel as a whole, is thereby raised in a radical way.

This has the immediate effect of widening our discussion within chapter 6. The signs are, as it were, an externalization of the significance of Jesus himself, and both seeing and not-seeing him are complex and ambiguous things. To see is not necessarily to believe (36); and yet to see is a necessary concomitant, perhaps a presupposition, of faith (40). As far as this chapter is concerned, the matter comes to a head in the difficult and disputed verse 62:

> Jesus knew in himself that his disciples were complaining about this, and said to them, Does this offend you? What then if you see the Son of man ascending where he was before?

I have argued elsewhere that the meaning of this verse is neither "If you see this, the offence will become greater than ever", nor "If you see this, the offence will be removed". The one event is both a heightening and the removal of the offence: the Son of man ascends by way of the cross, where the offence is both intensified and dissolved; crucifixion is glory. To this I would add, with reference to the theme now under discussion, that what is meant could be paraphrased: What if you see the Son of man becoming invisible, unseen? For when the Son of man ascends where he was before, he is no more visible than he was before the incarnation.

This tension of visibility and invisibility is central in John's thought; faith depends on sight, yet it is independent of sight, and cannot be equated with sight. This is a theme which, if time permitted, could be traced through the Gospel as a whole. It must suffice to quote the most important verse of all:

> It is because you have seen me that you have believed; blessed are those who have not seen, yet have believed (20.29).

Faith rests upon the once-for-all visibility of the Son of man, and especially of the risen Jesus; yet it is not simply observation, for to observe bare facts about Jesus (as in 6.42) can lead to unbelief, and faith itself means trust in the invisible—the invisible truth in the visible man Jesus, and indeed in the Son of man when the Son of man is no longer an earthly visible but a heavenly invisible figure. The dialectic that begins with the tension between seeing and believing is used further to analyse the meaning of faith itself.

2. We began this study of the themes of chapter 6 with the word σημεῖον. There is another word that John uses for the acts of Jesus: ἔργον, work. This too occurs in chapter 6, though not in precisely this sense. Verses 27–31 contain the noun and also the cognate verb ἐργάζεσθαι. After claiming that the enthusiasm of the crowd is based not on signs, properly understood, but on the easy satisfaction of their physical hunger, Jesus says, "Do not work (ἐργάζεσθε) for perishable food, but for food which endures

unto eternal life, the food which the Son of man will give" (27). The crowd make the natural assumption that in order to secure eternal life they must "work the works" required by God, who alone is the source of life. They assume a plurality of works, and desire to know how they are to be performed (28). Jesus replies that there is only one work that God requires, and that this is faith in himself. This claim evokes a demand for a sign (29f). The word "sign" (rather than "work") is naturally used here, for what is in mind is some kind of demonstration; but the supplementary question, τί ἐργάζῃ; "What work do you do?" shows that the discussion of works continues (30), and that σημεῖα and ἔργα are virtually synonymous.

Here is a genuine piece of dialectic, in which the theme of "work" is thrown backwards and forwards, and is shaped and reshaped in the process. Jesus himself introduces the theme; it is wrongly taken, in a legalistic sense; Jesus replies that working is to be understood in terms of faith; and the crowd in turn replies, asking for a sign, and implying that if "works", in their sense, are to be replaced by faith, he, as the one in whom faith is to rest, must perform a work significant enough to support the faith of others who have no works of their own but only faith in him. Jesus' answer is found in the ensuing discourse on the Bread of Life. This discussion thus has the effect of bringing out another dialectical aspect of the meaning of faith. Faith is, and is not, sight; faith is, and is not, work. These two propositions are both saved from degenerating into meaningless paradox because both come to rest in the person of Jesus himself, the place where, once for all, and for a moment in time, the invisible became visible, and the work of God was done—for the whole of the ensuing discourse brings out the fact that Jesus is the bread of life precisely because he came not to do his own will but the will of the Father who sent him (38), and in this obedience to offer his own flesh for the life of the world (51). This might be put in other words in the proposition that faith is the theological term that expresses the dialectic of seeing and not seeing, of working and not working.

3. The passage about faith and works (verses 27–30) leads immediately, and naturally, to a reference to the Old Testament:

> What work do you do? Our fathers ate the manna in the wilderness, as it is written, He gave them bread from heaven to eat (30–1).

It is implied: Can you, to justify your claim to be the one sent by God as the focus for faith, do any work comparable with this act of Moses? The reply is given in verses 32–5; of these verses the first is awkwardly expressed. Literally it runs:

Not Moses has given you the bread from heaven, but my Father gives you the bread, the true bread from heaven.

In the first clause it is the name Moses that is negatived: οὐ Μωϋσῆς δέδωκεν ὑμῖν, and it seems that John is trying to express two thoughts. In the first place, he accepts the statement of the Psalm: the supernatural wilderness food was bread from heaven. But it was not Moses who gave it; it is implied, it was the gift of God, and Moses was no more than an agent in its transmission. Secondly, however, the manna, though given by God himself, was not the true (ἀληθινός) bread from heaven; this (as the following verses make clear) is to be found only in Jesus, the one who himself came down from heaven.

In this short paragraph the attitude of John to the Old Testament is brought out, though so briefly and allusively that I must not here attempt to develop it at length. This could be done only by ranging much more widely in the Gospel. The initial proposition from which the dialogue begins is that which is ascribed to the Jews: the Old Testament is a possession of their own, which provides a foundation for their claims—it was to their fathers that Moses gave the heavenly bread, they themselves are the heirs of Abraham, and in searching the Scriptures they possess eternal life. But in fact (so the Johannine counter runs) the Old Testament is not essentially about Moses and Abraham, but about God, who alone, and always, is the giver of life; moreover, though God did do great things for his people through Abraham and Moses, what he did through them is only a secondary pointer to what he is now doing and giving in Jesus. Hence it is not wrong to search the Scriptures (5.39), but the only significant result of the process is to perceive that they bear witness to Jesus, and so to come to him. 6.32 is thus a dialectical statement and summary of John's understanding of the Old Testament.

4. A fourth theme of great importance arises as follows. I have just used the phrase, "come to Jesus". This occurs several times in both literal and metaphorical senses (which tend to run into each other).

Jesus saw that a large crowd was coming to him, and said to Philip, Where are we to buy bread that these people may eat? (5).

Jesus knew that they were going to come and seize him, to make him a king (15).

The crowd embarked and came to Capernaum, looking for Jesus (24).

He who comes to me shall not hunger, and he who believes in me shall never thirst (35).

Him who comes to me I will certainly not cast out (37).

So far the material is straightforward. The crowds are impressed by Jesus and repeatedly come to him, to hear his words, to receive the benefit of free meals, to be awed by his miraculous works. At the same time they wish to confer benefits upon him. Convinced that he is already a prophet they wish to make him king. He refuses their favours, but is ready to gratify their need, and feeds the multitude in the desert. This readiness is expressed in another way when Jesus comes to his disciples, threatened by the rising wind in the middle of the sea. His readiness to give is not confined to physical food; he himself is the bread of life and gives himself to those who come, with the result that spiritual hunger and thirst are satisfied. None is refused; whoever comes is received. It is at this point that the line of thought takes a fresh turn. This turn is already indicated in verse 37, where the open promise to everyone who comes is prefaced by the statement, "All ($\pi\hat{a}\nu$) that the Father gives me shall come to me". The corresponding negative, that only what the Father gives will come, is not stated, but it is implied, and the implication is confirmed in the remaining passages.

No one can come to me unless the Father who sent me draws him (44).

Every one who has heard from the Father and learned (from him) comes to me (45).

Jesus knew from the beginning who they were who did not believe, and who it was who should betray him. And he said,

This is why I said to you that no one could come to me unless it were given him from the Father (64–5).

The fact is that this chapter (and it would be possible to expand the discussion to cover the whole Gospel) contains material that suggests that it lies within the competence of man freely to make up his mind to come to Jesus and thus to receive at his hand the gift of life that he offers without distinction or reservation, and that equally it contains material that suggests that this coming lies wholly within the freedom of God, who alone determines who shall come to Jesus. The double theme is crystallized at the end of the chapter, when Jesus asks the Twelve whether they, like others, mean to desert him. Peter replies as if the choice were entirely in the disciples' hands. They have discovered that the words of Jesus convey eternal life; they have reached the conclusion that Jesus is the Holy One of God. In this Peter is wrong: the Twelve have not chosen Jesus, but he has chosen them; moreover, to underline the irrelevance of their self-determination, one of them is a devil, who will betray Jesus (70f). This corrects, but it does not obliterate, the confession of faith made so emphatically in verses 68f.

The fact is that John approaches the doctrine of predestination in the only tolerable way; and that way is dialectical. It is a doctrine that has suffered through alternative forms of statement, produced respectively by rationalization and mythologization. On the whole the mythological kind of restatement has prevailed in the history of Christian thought: it has produced, for example, the dispute between the infralapsarian and supralapsarian views of election, and above all the "horrible decree", which, out of a total human population of n, consigns x to inevitable bliss and $(n-x)$ to inevitable woe. Rationalization tends to end in either universalism or determinism. Predestination is in fact a dialogue between God and man, though it is one in which God, because he is God, will always have the last word. Seeing is not necessarily believing, coming is not necessarily believing, for the faith that unites with Christ and receives the gift of life is not a human property. Effective coming means being drawn by God (44); effective seeing means being taught by God (45). Yet, when this is said, the seeing is real seeing, the coming real coming, and the believing real believing, man's seeing, man's coming, man's believing. The course of the Gospel as a whole (and chapter 6 forms an excellent microcosm of it) shows Jesus engaged in dialogue with disciples, potential and actual; and it is only at the end that it is disclosed that "You did not choose me, but I chose you" (15.16).

5. What I have just said will serve to introduce the last in this series of themes. Chapter 6 contains a variety of propositions with regard to Christology: the sealing of the Son (27), the first use of ἐγώ εἰμι (35), the term Son of man. No less important than these is the movement of the narrative. At the beginning of the chapter the crowds are impressed and attracted. This responsive attitude increases up to the point at which they make a baffled attempt to seize Jesus and set him up as king. From this point the tide turns, until many even of his professed disciples follow him no more (66). They leave him because he has offered more than they asked; not places in a king's court, but personal union with himself.

It may be said that the essentials of a dialectical Christology are already laid down in the familiar words of 1.14: ὁ λόγος σὰρξ ἐγένετο. The Word is God, yet becomes not merely man but flesh. But, as we saw, dialectic means more than the existence of anti-thetical propositions; it involves discourse, so that it would not be wrong to say that it is already implied in the use of the term λόγος, and the whole Gospel, not least chapter 6, can be seen as a working out of this implication; it is God's discourse with man. It is an over-simplification of the Johannine representation of the ministry if we speak simply of Word and flesh, of a divine nature and a human nature, distinct yet united in one person. I do not say that this is christologically false, but it can easily lead to the barren and mechanical sort of picture, worked out—I was about to say, with Heath-Robinson elaboration—in, for example, Leo's *Tome*: "Unum horum coruscat miraculis, aliud succumbit injuriis." It would accord better with John's narrative to speak of a revealing and a non-revealing aspect of Jesus' ministry. We return here from a different angle to the theme of predestination. One and the same Christ is seen from different viewpoints by different persons with different results. A dialectical Christology, such as John's, is not a dissection of a static Christ, but the analysis of a living, moving, speaking Christ, or rather of the relation between this living figure and his environment. I have neither time nor ability to work this out in terms of systematic theology, but it seems to me that there is a task here for those who are competent to undertake it. Exegetically, we may see here the right way to handle the material which Dr Käsemann uses in support of his view that John's Christology is docetic.

I must return to the familiar theological and critical problems that I mentioned at the outset. We now have before us a theological setting in which the material relating to eschatology and to the Supper may be understood. It is not merely that John's eschatology had both present and futuristic elements. The coexistence of these elements is a feature of New Testament thought in general, and constitutes one of its unavoidable problems. What John offers us is a special means of elucidating the relation between them. At times he can simply and sharply set them side by side: "The hour cometh and now is" (4.23; 5.25). But in chapter 6 he allows them to appear in dialogue—in dialectic. The believer, he who comes to me, he who eats, has eternal life; but he does not have it in such a way that he himself becomes a self-contained source of life. His life consists in his being raised up by Christ, and it will never consist in anything else. This is the Christian contradiction of the famous words of Faust:

> Zum Augenblicke dürft' ich sagen,
> Verweile doch, du bist so schön!

There is no moment so fair that the Christian is justified in desiring that it may be made permanent. There is an "infinite qualitative distinction between time and eternity", and the boundary is one that may not be crossed. This observation is crucial for the understanding of Johannine theology, and of John's purpose and method in writing his Gospel. Not only the moments of religious experience, splendid, convincing, and exalting as they may be, stand under the dialectic of "I will raise him up at the last day", but also the supreme moment of the ministry of Jesus. "It is expedient for you that I go away" (16.7); it is expedient, that is, that the moment occupied by the ministry of Jesus, though this is the crucial historical manifestation of the truth of God, should come and go: "Blessed are those who have not seen" (20.29); "Greater works than these shall he do" (14.12). The Fourth Gospel could only have been written by one who regarded the life, death, and resurrection of Jesus as the indispensable turning-point in God's dealing with mankind; but the evangelist does not look upon this complex event in an historicistic way, treating it either as the climax of a play, to be followed by a resolution, or as a vanished golden age, nostalgically longed for. He views it dialectically, as a moment of disclosure but equally as a moment of concealment (12.36–40), and this dialectic is pushed forward into the continuing future, in which men continue to live under the necessity of that same decision of faith which was once evoked by sight and is now demanded by the apostolic testimony and the witness of the Spirit (16.8–11). The mark of this continuing dialectic is given in the reference to "the last day".

When this is grasped, the problem of the oblique eucharistic references in verses 51–8 can be grasped too. It is not by accident that this paragraph too contains (54) a reference to the last day, and Dr Bultmann seems to me to be nearly but not quite right in his view that the eucharistic and eschatological references come into the Gospel together as a piece of ecclesiastical redaction. They do belong together, not, however, as a corruption but as an example of the Johannine reinterpretation of Christian theology. What was said above about the historical moment of the life of Jesus, and the moments of religious experience, is true also of eucharistic communion. He who eats the flesh and drinks the blood of the Son of man has life, but he does not have it as a personal possession which he holds in his own right; he will never cease to need what is expressed in the words, "I will raise him up at the last day". There is thus a radical difference between this Johannine paragraph and the Ignatian φάρμακον ἀθανασίας, the ἀντίδοτος τοῦ μὴ ἀποθανεῖν. The Lord's Supper is thus neither a bare historical commemoration of an interesting and impressive event in the life of Jesus, nor an independent automatic means of conveying spiritual sustenance. It is part of the dialectic of time and eternity, of matter and spirit (cf. verse 63), in which the "night in which he was betrayed", and the "last day" each play their significant roles.

The words I have just used will enable me to draw this study to a close. John has removed what we call the "words of institution" from the Last Supper and alluded to them here, because this remarkable chapter, and the discourse on the Bread of Life, provide the dialectical framework in which the Supper can be rightly understood. In doing this, however, he was not introducing a new theme, but making explicit, and at great depth, what was already present in the traditional material. The oldest account of the Supper that we possess includes the words,

> As often as you eat this loaf and drink the cup you proclaim the Lord's death, until he come (1 Cor. 11.26).

The Supper, as Christians observe it, takes place between the historical event of the Lord's death, to which it looks back, and the meta-historical event of the Lord's coming, to which it looks forward. The specific motivation for the inclusion of the paragraph 51–8 may well have been the reference to thirst (as well as hunger) in verse 35; but the essential motivation was John's insight into the older tradition.

This example points out the general setting and direction of John's theological work. He perceived, as few of his contemporaries did, the turbulent dialectic of the primitive Christian tradition, and of the life of Jesus himself. The tendency to simplify—to simplify in the wrong way—was early present in Christian circles. It was easy on the one hand to formulate a series of *acta* and *decreta* of Jesus and the apostles which could be used as a new Christian law handed down as accurately as possible from one generation to another by authorized tradents; easy on the other hand to use the name of Jesus and a certain amount of Christian terminology as a cloak for a body of free gnostic speculation. Whatever Johannine theology is, it is neither bald historicism nor unbridled gnosis. It represents rather a creative and perceptive handling of the earlier tradition, free in that it addresses to the basic Christian conviction whatever new questions a new age might suggest, obedient in that it is bound to the original apostolic witness to Jesus. The "dialectical theology of St John" is not a novel invention, but an authentic insight into the meaning of Christian origins.

Whether this Johannine dialectic arose through external circumstances such as those so persuasively described by Dr J. L. Martyn, or within the mind of John himself, is a question we have no means of answering decisively. Probably the right answer is, Both. That John had the original and creative mind—the Socratic mind that is capable of asking itself questions, and arguing with itself—is written on every page of the Gospel; that he never disputed with Jews, Greeks, and his fellow-Christians, seems highly improbable. But in the last resort Johannine theology was created neither by

John's mind nor by the circumstances at the end of the first century, nor by any combination of these. It was created by the historic event and the witness of the Spirit. And while the Gospel itself presents us with many other components of a dialectical theology—life and death, truth and error, light and darkness, flesh and spirit, sight and blindness, love and hate—it is in this tension (which incidentally points the way to a reconciliation between dialectical and kerygmatic) that Christian dialectical theology arises.

5

The Acts—of the Apostles

The Acts of the Apostles: the familiar title raises immediately the question, Who were the apostles whose acts are here described? The question must not be pressed too hard, for the title as we have it, πράξεις ἀποστόλων, was not an original part of the book itself. It is, however, very old. It is contained in every manuscript, except Codex Sinaiticus, which has the one word, Acts, πράξεις, and was already customary in the second half of the second century. It is found, for example, in the well-known Anti-Marcionite Prologue to the Third Gospel: "And subsequently the same Luke wrote the Acts of the Apostles." It occurs, slightly expanded, in the Muratorian Canon: "The acts of all the apostles have been written in one book." It is evident that our book is not an account of the acts of all the apostles, *acta omnium apostolorum*; in describing it so the Muratorian List is certainly mistaken. But the List presupposes the simple title, *Acta Apostolorum*, and explains, probably with polemical intent, that there was not one apostle only, Paul, as Marcion believed, but a plurality of apostles. Tertullian, also, who defends the canonical authority of Acts against Marcion[1] uses the title *Acta Apostolorum*. So far as I can see, Irenaeus does not use it; and it seems not improbable that it originated in the Anti-Marcionite conflicts of the middle of the second century. It may well have been at this time that Luke's two volumes were separated from each other, the first drawn into the four Gospel canon, and the second used to demonstrate the unity of Paul with the Jerusalem Church, at the same time acquiring its new title.

The Anti-Marcionite argument, as we encounter it in, for example, Tertullian, is not always logically convincing. It is apt to fall into some such pattern as the following:

(*a*) This book describes the words and deeds of the Twelve Apostles; therefore it is apostolic and canonical.

[1] *Adv. Marcionem* 5. 2, 3; *De Praescr.* 22, 23.

(*b*) This book has been shown to be apostolic and canonical; therefore all the Twelve, and not (as Marcion supposes) Paul only, are apostles.

This circular argument is not likely to persuade an unbiased reader; it may, however, serve to confirm the observation that no one can read Acts without asking the question, Who were the apostles?[1]

Acts is not the only book in the New Testament that evokes this question; it arises also in the companion volume, the Gospel according to Luke. Mark uses the word ἀπόστολος only once (6.30), and here it has no technical significance. Mark could equally well have used a passive participle of the verb "to send" (ἀπεσταλμένοι or ἀποσταλέντες): "Those who had been sent out came back." Luke, however, uses the word six times (6.13; 9.10; 11.49; 17.5; 22.14; 24.10), and it is clear that in the Third Gospel the apostles form a clearly defined and delimited group. There are only twelve apostles; the seventy (or seventy-two), who according to Luke 10.1 were sent out by Jesus, are never described as apostles, though their commissioning is entirely similar to that of the Twelve. It is naturally to the Twelve, and to the Twelve only, that the promise applies that they shall sit on thrones judging the twelve tribes of Israel (22.30). The Twelve Apostles are the primary witnesses of the resurrection—not the only witnesses, for Luke makes it clear that the risen Jesus appeared to the Eleven and those who were with them (24.33: οἱ ἕνδεκα καὶ οἱ σὺν αὐτοῖς; cf. 1 Cor. 15.6f); but there can be no doubt that here too the Twelve are the really significant and indispensable figures.

This fact is clear enough in Luke; but it is underlined and made even clearer in Acts, where the leading role of the Twelve Apostles stands out unmistakably. It is to them that the risen Christ shows himself in a sequence of resurrection appearances (1.3), and it is emphatically repeated that they have been chosen through an act of divine inspiration (1.2, διὰ πνεύματος ἁγίου). It is promised that they in turn shall receive the gift of the Holy Spirit (1.4, 5, 8), and thus become the empowered and authorized witnesses of Jesus from Jerusalem to the end of the world (1.8). Both their own

---

[1] I have dealt with this question at greater length in my Cato Lecture, *The Signs of an Apostle* (1970). In the present context I am pursuing it not for its own sake but as an approach to the problems of Acts, so that the overlap between the two discussions is slight.

unique importance as a closed group, and the importance of the number twelve, by which they are limited, are underlined by the narrative of the election of Matthias, to which I shall return later in this chapter. When the promise of the gift of the Spirit is fulfilled on the Day of Pentecost, it is Peter with the Eleven who explains to the assembled multitude the meaning of the supernatural event that they have witnessed (2.14). After this, the number twelve is mentioned only once more (6.2), but "the apostles" (and certainly in the sense of "the twelve apostles") are referred to in all twenty-six times—for the last time in 16.4. They preach, they work miracles, they teach, they are arrested and thrown into prison, they receive gifts for the support of the poor, they appoint others to carry out this task of the relief of distress. In view of this central place that Luke accords to the Twelve Apostles it is the more striking that he has so little specific information about them. He has a few narratives about Peter (into some of which John is brought in a non-speaking, almost non-acting, role), and records the martyrdom of James; in addition he has no information to impart about any of the Twelve—save that he existed, and was one of the Twelve. If one reads quickly and superficially through the first fifteen chapters of Acts, one gains the impression, This book is indeed πράξεις ἀποστόλων, the acts of the apostles. But a second, slower reading cannot fail to raise the question, But who in fact were these apostles, and what did it mean to them to be apostles? Luke provides us with twelve names (eleven in 1.13, supplemented at 1.26 by that of Matthias), but what do we know about the men who bore them?

It is not only in Acts that this problem arises. It is in this setting, for example, that the question about the opponents referred to by Paul in 2 Corinthians 10–13 arises. This is one of the most important questions in the study of the New Testament,[1] with extensive repercussions both historical and theological. In these chapters we meet "false apostles" (ψευδαπόστολοι) and "super-apostles" (ὑπερλίαν ἀπόστολοι), against whom Paul defends himself and his office. This, however, is only part—though a vital part—of a wider question. It is disputed whether the opponents we meet in these four chapters are the same as those we meet in other Pauline letters, notably Galatians; from the epistles as a whole, however, the following propositions stand out with complete certainty: no

[1] See my paper in *New Testament Studies* 17 (1971), pp. 233–54.

one was more confident than Paul that he was an apostle; this confidence of Paul's was attacked, so that his apostleship was sometimes accepted, sometimes denied; no one had a more profound
understanding than Paul of the nature and meaning of apostleship;
others who also claimed to be apostles had a different conception of
what apostleship meant. I have discussed these points elsewhere,
and shall refer to them again later in this chapter; for the moment it
is sufficient to note that the question, Who were the apostles?
which is thrown up by the reading of Acts, arises again in the study
of the Pauline letters. Paul himself, according to his own conviction, is an apostle. Others make the same claim for themselves;
among them are some who deny Paul's apostleship, some whom he
regards as no better than false apostles. Who then were the
apostles?

Other pieces of early Christian literature give rise to somewhat
different forms of the same question. Thus the Apocalypse
emphasizes the central and unique importance of the Twelve
Apostles as heavily as any book in the New Testament: their
names are written on the twelve foundations of the Holy City
(21.14; cf. Eph. 2.20). This means that the apostolate is a closed
group, and that there can therefore be no question who does and
who does not belong to it; one either is or is not in the list—Peter,
Andrew, James, John, and so on. But in Revelation 2.2 we
encounter those who profess to be apostles but are not. This means
not only that there exist (as Paul had said) "false apostles", but
also that a second definition of the word "apostle" is current. As I
have observed, if the claim, I am an apostle, means, I am Peter, or
Andrew, or some other of a small and strictly limited group, it is
one that can be checked at once, and could very seldom be falsely
made with any show of plausibility. The fact that the claim was
made shows that the category "apostle" had a wider connotation,
sufficiently broad for a stranger to be able to make the claim, I am
an apostle, with at least some hope of being believed. A similar
variation is attested by the *Didache*. The full title of this little
book is, "The Teaching of the Lord through the Twelve Apostles".
Here "apostle" has its narrow, delimited sense. In the course of
the book, however, it is used otherwise:

Let every apostle who comes to you be received as the Lord.
He shall not stay more than one day, though if there be need he

F

may stay a second also. But if he stays three, he is a false prophet. When the apostle leaves, let him take nothing but a loaf, to last till he next finds lodging; if he asks for money, he is a false prophet (11.4ff).

This apostle is evidently not one of the original group, appointed by the Lord himself during his ministry, but a wandering preacher, whose bona fides must be carefully scrutinized. These wandering preachers, at least under the name *apostle*, died out fairly early. In the writings of Clement of Rome and of Ignatius of Antioch "the apostles" are already a closed circle with unique authority.

The apostles received the Gospel for us from the Lord Jesus Christ; Jesus Christ was sent forth from God. So Christ is from God, and the apostles are from Christ; both missions took place in good order in fulfilment of the will of God (1 Clement 42.1f).

Similarly let all men respect the deacons as Jesus Christ, as also they should respect the bishop as a type of the Father, and the elders as God's council and as the band of the apostles; without these nothing can be called a church . . . Out of my love for you I am thus sparing you, although I could write more urgently on his [the bishop's] behalf; but I did not consider myself sufficient, condemned man that I am, to order you as if I were an apostle (Ignatius, *Trallians* 3).

I have quoted the passage from Ignatius at some length in order to show both that Ignatius thought of the apostles as a closed college (σύνδεσμος), and that he sharply distinguishes between himself and them. For Clement and for Ignatius the apostles were the first rulers of the Church, and the source of right doctrine and right order. The further development of thought about the apostles in the second century need not be considered here.[1]

It is not my intention in this chapter to study the origin and significance of the primitive Christian apostolate. But I note the pioneering work in this field of K. H. Rengstorf,[2] whose inquiries have been followed up (though not always, in my opinion, in the

---

[1] See "The Apostles in and after the New Testament", in *Svensk Exegetisk Årsbok* xxi (1956), pp. 30–49.

[2] K. H. Rengstorf, *Apostolat und Predigtamt* (Stuttgart 1934; 2nd edn, 1954); also the article ἀποστέλλω, κτλ. in G. Kittel, *TWNT* i,pp. 397–448.

right direction) by, among others, G. Klein[1] and W. Schmithals.[2] According to Dr Klein, the origin of the notion of "the twelve apostles" is to be found in the Lucan writings; Luke developed it out of the earlier Pauline conception of the apostolate. In some respects Dr Schmithals agrees, but thinks that "Luke found his concept of the apostles already in existence" (p. 273), and that the origin of the Lucan concept is to be found in that of the gnostic missionary.[3] There is a wide field of investigation before us here; we need it, however, only in order to provide a point of departure for the study of Acts.

The fact is that the earliest Christian documents to use the word "apostle" are the Pauline letters. From the literary point of view Paul must be regarded as the origin of the Christian concept of apostleship. He was not, however, the first apostle, for he himself refers to those who were apostles before him (Gal. 1.17: τοὺς πρὸ ἐμοῦ ἀποστόλους), and reports that after the resurrection the Lord appeared to the Twelve and to all the apostles before he appeared to him (1 Cor. 15.5–8). This, it will be observed, does not necessarily or even probably mean that, in Paul's view, "the Twelve" and "the Apostles" were terms of identical meaning. It is further to be observed that even the servants of Satan can disguise themselves as apostles of Christ (2 Cor. 11.13: μετασχηματίζονται εἰς ἀποστόλους Χριστοῦ); this (like Rev. 2.2, referred to above) presupposes that ἀπόστολος was already a recognized category; if there were false apostles, ψευδαπόστολοι, there must have been also genuine apostles, whom it was possible to imitate. Again, it must not be concluded from this that there must have been twelve and only twelve genuine apostles; as we have seen, the opposite is more likely to be true. Peter, nevertheless, was one of these apostles (Gal. 1.18f), and Paul asserts not only an important distinction but also a fundamental similarity between Peter and himself when he writes that "he who was at work in Peter to produce an apostolate for the circumcised was at work also in me for the Gentiles" (Gal. 2.8). This verse registers an agreement

---

[1] *Die zwölf Apostel, Ursprung und Gehalt einer Idee*, FRLANT, NF 59 (Göttingen 1961).

[2] *Das kirchliche Apostelamt, eine historische Untersuchung*, FRLANT, NF 61 (Göttingen 1961).

[3] See a particular development of this theme in D. Georgi, *Die Gegner des Paulus im 2. Korintherbrief*, WMANT 11 (Neukirchen 1964).

reached in discussion between Paul and the "Pillars" in Jerusalem, but whether Peter understood the agreement, that is, whether he understood his apostolate, in the same way as Paul is doubtful. Whether indeed anyone can be shown to have shared Paul's conception of apostleship is doubtful. We cannot with certainty deduce Peter's own view of the matter from the narrative of Acts, or from chance observations in the Pauline letters; Luke's view of the position of the primitive apostles will be considered later. Paul probably tended to assume that Peter would understand his vocation as an apostle in the same way that he, Paul, understood his. He did, however, know that Peter practised apostleship in a different way; for example, Peter made use of the apostolic privilege of taking his wife with him on his journeys at the expense of the Churches to which he travelled (1 Cor. 9.5); Paul preferred to renounce such rights.

This observation leads us to the heart of the matter. Paul, as one called to be an apostle, κλητὸς ἀπόστολος (Rom. 1.1), was, as Fridrichsen put it,[1] an "eschatologic person", playing a significant role of his own in the events of the last days. He understood his eschatological role to mean that he must spread the gospel as widely as possible before the coming of the Lord.[2] That is to say, for Paul an apostle[3] is a missionary, and essentially a pioneer missionary (cf. Rom. 15.20; 2 Cor. 10.12–16). And to be a missionary means to proclaim the word of the cross (ὁ λόγος ὁ τοῦ σταυροῦ, 1 Cor. 1.18); and to proclaim the word of the cross means not only to preach, but also to carry about in the body the dying of Jesus (τὴν νέκρωσιν τοῦ Ἰησοῦ, 2 Cor. 4.10). Out of his understanding of his apostolic office arose not only the content of his preaching but also his manner of life. The preacher of the cross could not be an authoritarian, still less a violent, person, and though Paul could perform the signs of an apostle (2 Cor. 12.12) in the sense of miracles—σημεῖά τε καὶ τέρατα καὶ δυνάμεις—the most complete and satisfactory sign of his apostleship was his humiliation. An apostleship of this kind, understood in this way, Paul could have received from no human authority; it was only, and directly, from the crucified Christ (Χριστὸς ἐσταυρωμένος,

---

[1] *The Apostle and his Message* (Uppsala 1947), p. 3.

[2] It may be that this gave his Gentile mission special significance. "The fullness of the Gentiles" must first be brought in as a condition for the salvation of Israel (Rom. 11.25f).

[3] This was certainly not the primary meaning of the Hebrew *šaliaḥ*.

1 Cor. 1.23) that he could receive the honour of being one of the ἐπιθανάτιοι (1 Cor. 4.9), one of those under sentence of death, a spectacle exposed to the mockery of men and angels.

From this Pauline picture of an apostle we return to Acts. How does Luke describe the apostles and their work?

We have already seen that Luke identifies the apostolic group, active in the early years of the primitive Church, with the Twelve, whose election and appointment by Jesus himself are described in the Gospel tradition. Of the defection of Judas, and his replacement by Matthias, and of the death of James, and his replacement by—no one, I shall have to speak later. The continuity between the personal disciples of Jesus during his ministry and the apostolic founders of the Church is of great importance for Luke who underlines it in 1.21: the apostles are witnesses of the resurrection not only in the sense that they have seen the risen Christ, but also in that they are able to establish the identity of the Risen One with the Jesus whose life and teaching are recounted in the Gospel. It follows from this direct contact and continuity that their ministry is also in some sense his ministry. The Gospel narrates that which he began to do and to teach (Acts. 1.1), Acts that which he continued to do and to teach through the Holy Spirit whom he bestowed upon the Church. As Jesus personally was Lord for the group of disciples that accompanied him, so his representatives exercise leadership in the new community that came into being as a result of his resurrection. Through their preaching the Church was called into being, through their teaching it is instructed. No one is able to withstand them. When they are cast into prison, they are delivered by angels. The Jewish Council cannot put them to silence, and the common people are deeply impressed by their beneficent and punitive miracles. They appoint others to perform necessary tasks in the community, and decide important questions in doctrine and ethics. Their preaching is heard and accepted by thousands. All this seems to be far removed from the Pauline picture of the ἐπιθανάτιοι, the men who live under sentence of death. But of course it is true that I have not given a complete account of the apostles as they appear in Acts. They can be delivered from prison only because they have first been cast into prison; they are scourged; James is killed with the sword; and Paul, who is one of the apostolic company, the mightiest preacher of them all, before whom even Roman officials are converted or at least show themselves not unfavourable to the new movement, is scourged, stoned, and imprisoned; he suffers shipwreck, and teaches that it is through many tribulations that we must enter the kingdom of God (14.22). Yet, when all is said, in Luke's view it is the deliverance rather than the sufferings that demonstrates the apostolicity of the apostles, and the difference between the Pauline and Lucan conceptions of apostleship is considerable. In Acts, the apostles are the eminent leaders of the Christian circle, whose divine authorization is visible, or at least should be visible, to the impartial observer. With Paul it is different.

The difference between Acts and Paul can be illuminated by two examples. The first is the election, or co-option, of Matthias to fill the place left vacant by Judas. Two points are particularly important.

1. It is assumed to be necessary that there should be twelve apostles, neither more nor fewer; that is, Luke has equated "the twelve" and "the apostles" without remainder. The significance of the number twelve is never explained in Acts[1]; this makes the enphasis placed upon it the more impressive. It is simply assumed, and proved from Scripture (1.20, citing Ps. 109.8), that when one of the Twelve defects someone else must take his place—the number must be made up. So far as we are right in seeing in the election of Matthias an historical event, Professor Rengstorf is right in explaining it within the framework of the messiahship of Jesus and the eschatological hope of the redemption of Israel. He writes:

> Even though Judas has lost his *klēros*, the calling of Israel to the Kingdom of God has not become invalid. On the contrary, the calling remains; for Jesus is the Messiah (2.36), and this in its turn means that *he is* the promised king of Israel. As during the lifetime of Jesus, so now, the gospel is to be proclaimed to Israel. In this way Luke shows clearly that he does not want to see anything changed in that scheme of redemption according to which the gospel is *first* meant for the Jews.[2]

[1] See the important Q saying: Matt. 19.28 = Luke 22.30.

[2] K. H. Rengstorf, "The Election of Matthias", in *Current Issues in New Testament Interpretation: Essays in Honor of O. A. Piper* (New York (also London) 1962), pp. 178–92; quotation from p. 189. I have corrected the reference (Acts 2.36). There is a fuller German version of this paper in *Studia Theologica* xv (1961), pp. 35–67.

Since the circle of twelve is certainly pre-Pauline (1 Cor. 15.5), and since the betrayal by Judas possesses very high historical probability, and since the Twelve showed almost no inclination to set about a Gentile mission, it may well be that this was the original meaning of the Matthias story. Luke, however, does not seem to have seen, and certainly does not interpret, the narrative so clearly, and its meaning has to be drawn out from quite small and apparently fortuitous pieces of evidence. Luke does not repeat in Acts the Q passage (Luke 22.30 = Matt. 19.28) which decisively connects the Twelve with the twelve tribes of Israel, that is, the complete and renewed[1] people of God of the last days. He clings, however, to the conviction that the Twelve were the original group of apostles, appointed by Jesus himself, that the purpose of their appointment was eschatological, and that for this reason there had to be twelve (and not, say, eleven or thirteen) of them.

2. Their eschatological purpose now, however, in Acts, looks somewhat different. The Twelve were the indispensable link that held together the historical Jesus (1.21), the risen Lord (1.22), and the Church; but this, in Luke's view, they were for the benefit not only of the Jews but of the Gentiles too. This is shown by his repetition of the substance of 1.22 in 10.39, in Peter's speech before Cornelius and his Gentile friends; there too it is pointed out that the apostles, the chosen witnesses, could vouch not only for the resurrection of Jesus, but also for "all the things he did both in the land of the Jews and in Jerusalem". Luke, as author of the Third Gospel as well as of Acts, had at his disposal two bodies of traditional material, a "Twelve-tradition" and an "Apostle-tradition". These he united by identifying the two groups (which Paul, writing at a date nearer to the events, appears in 1 Corinthians 15.5,7 to have distinguished). The identification was in the first instance a literary procedure, but its historical effect was to bind together as tightly as possible the Gospel story of Jesus and the development of the Church. It facilitated this literary procedure on Luke's part that he possessed also an historical tradition about Matthias, which he used probably without fully understanding its original significance.

[1] Note Matthew's παλιγγενεσία.

Luke's use of the Matthias tradition leads to the second example which sheds light on his understanding of the apostles, and thus of his historical and theological task. The addition of the otherwise unknown and historically insignificant Matthias to the apostolic group as its twelfth member underlines the fact that, even after the death of James, Paul was not so added. To the much debated question of the Paulinism of Acts I shall return in the next chapter; here we must simply observe that Paul, who defended his apostleship so passionately, is in Acts no apostle at all.

It is true that Paul and Barnabas appear to be described as apostles in Acts 14.4,14. In Iconium, after Paul and Barnabas had preached there, the Jews stirred up feeling against them, and "the population of the city was divided; some sided with the Jews, others with the apostles". In Lystra, when "the apostles Barnabas and Paul" heard that it was intended to offer sacrifice to them as gods, "they tore their clothes, sprang into the crowd, and shouted, Men, why are you doing this?" Apart from these verses Paul is never in Acts referred to as an apostle. How are the exceptions to be explained? Explanations of a literary kind have been attempted. Thus it has often been claimed that at 14.14 Luke was following a written source, in which Paul and Barnabas were described as apostles. He mechanically followed the wording of this source, without noticing that it contradicted his usual practice and belief. The wording of verse 14 then in some way cast its influence backwards upon verse 4. This is not very convincing. A better suggestion begins from the observation that in verse 14 the Western Text[1] does not contain the word apostle, but runs simply, "When Barnabas and Paul heard . . ." (ἀκούσας δὲ Βαρναβᾶς καὶ Παῦλος). This, with its singular participle out of concord with the plural subject, is certainly the more difficult reading, and may well be original. If it is accepted, the word apostle disappears from verse 14, and in verse 4 it is capable of being given a different interpretation, which does not apply it directly to Barnabas and Paul: "Some took the Jewish, others the apostolic (that is, the Christian) side". This reinterpretation of verse 4 is possible, but less convincing than the textual point in

---

[1] The word *apostles* is wanting in D *d gig h*; *pesh* also reads, "Barnabas and Paul, when they heard . . .". *h* at least did not remove the word on principle, for it includes it, against other witnesses, at 14.9.

verse 14. A further suggestion is that when Luke reached chapter 14 he felt that he had established the proper sense of "apostle" (that is, its equivalence with "member of the Twelve") so firmly that he could now afford to use it in a new, looser, sense, in order to make clear that Barnabas and Paul, though not in the strict sense apostles, were nevertheless apostolic men, closely associated with the apostles. This suggestion, however, does not explain why Luke used "apostle" in this wider sense twice in the first half of chapter 14, and never again in the remaining fourteen chapters of the book. The "explanations" are not really adequate (especially for 14.4), and the two verses remain as a problem. They are, however, exceptions, and must be treated as such, and it is the almost un-varying Lucan usage rather than the two exceptions that must be regarded as decisive. It is well known that there are in Acts a number of passages which on purely literary grounds have been described as unrevised[1]—the author has not (for whatever reason) succeeded in putting them into a shape with which he would himself have been fully satisfied. It may be so here. In the period in which Acts was written,[2] and indeed in what may be described as the Lucan circle, there were undoubtedly some to whom Paul was not merely an apostle but *the* apostle; it will suffice to mention the author of the Pastoral Epistles.[3] It is not necessary to adopt a questionable literary source theory to recog-nize that in Acts 14.4,14 this evaluation of Paul (and his col-leagues) shines through. Luke has not removed it, though it is contrary to his own conviction, according to which Paul was not an apostle, since he was not one of the only twelve apostles there were. Indeed, it is further possible that there was a division not only in the group of Deuteropaulinists of whom Luke was one but also in Luke's own mind. It is certain that he greatly admired and respected Paul—one might say, in his heart he thought of him as an apostle. It was his apostolic theory (which identified "the Apostles" with "the Twelve") that forbade him to describe

---

[1] It is hard to think that Luke intended such passages as 3.16; 10.36ff (to mention only the most striking) to remain as they are.

[2] It is not possible in this and the succeeding two chapters seriously to discuss the date of Acts; it seems probable that the book was written towards the close of the first century.

[3] See my commentary on the Pastoral Epistles, *New Clarendon Bible* (1963), pp. 16ff.

Paul as an apostle; and sometimes perhaps his heart got the better of his theory.

Luke's failure (as a rule) to describe Paul as an apostle does, however, emphasize the fact that there is a radical difference in form and content between the Lucan and Pauline conceptions of apostleship. For Luke, there are only twelve apostles, and Paul is not one of them. For Paul, there is no limited number of apostles, and his own place among them admits of no doubt. For Luke, the apostles are powerful, eminent, and distinguished figures. For Paul, they are the offscouring of the world, a spectacle to men and angels, never truer than when they are taken to be deceivers, never mightier than when they are weak. Some would make the distinction between the Lucan and Pauline concepts sharper still, seeing in Paul as depicted in Acts a subordinate figure, the first link between the apostles (that is, the Twelve) and the later Church. This goes too far; Luke shows no interest in formal succession, and evidently admires Paul far too much to give him a secondary position of this kind.

We must thus recognize that in the answering of a simple but central question, Who and what is an apostle? Luke and Paul are to be clearly distinguished. This is an astonishing paradox, for it is clear that Luke had the highest possible admiration for Paul. I shall return to this paradox and to the general question of the relation between Acts and Paul in the next chapter. For the present, the question before us is, What can we learn from these observations with regard to the origin and purpose of Acts, and for its interpretation?

1. It is evident that between Luke and Paul there is a great difference in theological profundity. If there is a *theologus gloriae*—one who thinks of Christianity as a cheerful climbing through the pearly gates to a not too inaccessible glory—to be found in the New Testament, it is Luke. In the Third Gospel the sufferings of Christ play a smaller part than they do in Mark, and in Acts the sufferings of the apostles play a smaller part than they do in Paul. Yet Luke used Mark, and it is certain that he thought of himself as on Paul's side, that he admired him greatly. This can only mean (and, as I have said, I shall return to this matter), not that Luke had any intention of contradicting or confuting the Pauline theology, but that he simply did not understand it at its full depth.

For him, Christian theology was not a theology of a suffering and rejected Christ, witnessed by a suffering and rejected apostle, but a simple message of the love of God, which all men of good will can accept, and will accept. Yet in saying this I have exaggerated the position. To describe Luke as a *theologus gloriae* is a grave over-simplification. Luke was an honest and sincere Christian, whose theology was concentrated upon Christ, and he knew quite well that the Christ who was the ground of his faith had been crucified. But the depths of his own christocentric theology he himself had not seen and understood, as Paul had seen and understood them. Later we shall encounter further examples of this fact, which will, I hope, illuminate it.

2. Luke wrote almost half a century later than Paul; Acts reflects the Christian situation at the end of the century. The years of pioneering were now over (it is in fact something of a wonder that so much ground was covered in so short a time); it was the time for consolidation. The process of consolidation was carried out in a variety of ways, and later we shall have to determine as precisely as we can the place of Acts within it. For the present it is sufficient to observe that the literary amalgamation of the "Twelve-tradition" with the "Apostles-tradition", which Luke carried out, was powerfully aided and accelerated by the theological and ecclesiastical necessity of finding a firm link between Jesus and the Church. Luke took over, perhaps he himself helped to form, the tradition that the Twelve, whom Jesus had appointed during his earthly ministry, became the leading and controlling members of the primitive Church. For him, the continuity thus established was, as we have seen, a necessary feature of the apostolic function (1.21; 10.39). It was Paul, or Paul's status, that suffered from this theory. A hero he might be (and to Luke he certainly was); an apostle he could not be. Paul suffered; but at the same time historical accuracy suffered too, for from the earlier documents it seems clear that among his contemporaries Paul was either an apostle, the greatest of apostles, or a nobody (2 Cor. 12.11), an abortion (1 Cor. 15.8)—certainly not a heroic non-apostle. This leads to a third point.

3. It would be easy—too easy—to draw from these facts and observations the conclusion that Luke simply misunderstood the

early history of Christianity and drew a misleading picture of it. This too would be an over-simplification. There are three factors that must be borne in mind at this point.

(*a*) Already in his own day Paul's apostleship came under attack. It is clear to any reader of the Pauline letters both that Paul firmly asserted his calling as an apostle, and that he was unable to prove it to the Church at large. He knew what it was to be scorned and rejected, not only by his enemies but also within his own Churches. If, as appears, Luke himself did not accept a contemporary claim (made, for example, by the author of the Pastorals) that Paul was an apostle, this was an end-of-the-century claim, and an end-of-the-century rejection; there was also a mid-century claim and a mid-century rejection— not the same as those current fifty years later, but not altogether unrelated to them.

(*b*) Paul himself attests not only the existence but also the importance of the Twelve (1 Cor. 15.5,11), of the Pillars (Gal. 2.9), of those who were apostles before him (Gal. 1.17). These groups were not invented by Luke, though he may have been mistaken in the way he identified them and related them to one another and to Paul.

(*c*) Paul also attests that, in addition to his own, other concepts of apostleship existed. Here we are to think not only of false apostles, ψευδαπόστολοι, who preached a different, and thus a false, gospel, but of those who were pleased to receive support from the churches, of those who built on foundations laid by others and made their way into churches they had not founded. These, moreover, were men of manifest power and importance; at least, they made a powerful impression on the Corinthians, and won from Paul the ironic titles, "Men with reputations", "Super-apostles".

All this means that the problems of Acts are in the first instance problems belonging to the end of the century, but they may also be seen as a reflection of the problems of the middle of the century. It is the crossing of these two ranges of problems that constitutes the greatest difficulty in the study of Acts. Each set of problems must be set out and grasped as if it stood alone, but also in relation to the other. Luke did not and could not write a straightforward record of events in the 30s, 40s, and 50s, because he was too well aware of what was going on in the 90s; but he was too conscientious in his relation to the earlier decades simply to transfer to them the circumstances of the later. It is in this light that Luke must be evaluated, whether as author, historian, or theologian. But the briefest of attempts at such evaluation must be deferred to the next two chapters.

6

The Acts—of Paul

It is probable that Acts was written towards the end of the first century. It is difficult to see how the Lucan picture of the apostles, as we traced it in Chapter 5 above, could have originated earlier than this. Other data point in the same direction, and many students of the book are agreed that it appeared at this time.[1] It is also clear (as we have seen) that the author was no profound theologian. In fact he was not so much a theologian as a pastor.[2] It is true that this is no absolute distinction; it is possible to be at the same time a pastor and a theologian—possible and indeed desirable, and it is to be hoped that all pastors should be capable theologians, and that professional theologians should not altogether forget their pastoral responsibilities. Nevertheless, there is a distinction, at least in emphasis, and Luke, it seems, did feel a pastoral responsibility for the situation of the Church of his time without fully understanding all the theological questions involved in this situation and this time.

The consequence of these facts is that neither the events nor the theology of the earliest Christian years can be made out from the pages of Acts with perfect clarity. This is not to say that Luke deliberately concealed the true story of the early years in order that his contemporaries might not know the shameful story of the conflicts of the past, or that he set out to produce a synthesis of its antithetical elements. For such purposes, even if he had desired to achieve them, Luke was simply not clever enough. Yet the result was in some respects the same as if he had carried out a tactful concealment or a philosophical scheme. The reader of Acts hears practically nothing of the conflicts which are familiar to us

[1] Other estimates range from the early 60s (Acts written in defence of Paul at his trial) to about 130 (Acts connected with Justin Martyr).

[2] See S. G. Wilson, *The Gentiles in the Gospel according to St Luke, and in the Acts of the Apostles*, a Durham thesis which is to be published in the S.N.T.S. Monograph Series.

from the Pauline letters. The mission to the Gentiles is held up only for a moment. The question about circumcision and other requirements of the Law is settled almost as soon as it is raised. Only the Jews, who had already (as Luke emphasizes both in the Third Gospel and in Acts) killed Jesus, disturb the peace of the Church, and even to them the opportunity of repentance and forgiveness is offered (for example, Acts 2.38f; 3.17,25f). Luke passes by in silence the problems of the Gentile mission and the bitterness of the circumcision controversy. He does this, however, not in the interests of a philosophical theory, but in order to build up the Church of his own age, and because, since he failed to see their theological point, he could see no edifying value in the story of the conflicts. He could, on the other hand, see very well that the Church of his day could learn much of value, both for its preaching and its living, from the example of "the good apostles" (as his contemporary Clement calls them), and the history that he writes is the history of a peaceful and orderly development. That is what things must have been like in the age of the apostles. If Luke has a theory to propagate, it is a theory of this kind about the apostles.

From this, and from the matters that were considered in the previous chapter, it follows that in the study of Acts there is no more important question than that of the "Paulinism" of the book. The only primary documents, contemporary with the events described in Acts, that we possess are the Pauline letters; the only participant in those events whom we know from first-hand, unassailable testimony is Paul. It is not surprising that practically everyone who in the last few years has written about Acts has concerned himself with this issue. We have dealt with one aspect of the question—the views of apostleship and the apostles found in Acts and in the Pauline letters respectively; we must now deal with the matter more generally, though still briefly; it will not be possible to look at more than a very few representative contributions.

The essay by P. Vielhauer, "On the 'Paulinism' of Acts", was first published in 1950[1]; since then it has appeared in English in the *Festschrift* for Paul Schubert.[2] In many respects this essay has determined the later discussion, both in form and in content.

[1] In *Evangelische Theologie* x, pp. 1–15.
[2] *Studies in Luke–Acts*, ed. L. E. Keck and J. L. Martyn (1968).

In order to make a comparison between the Paul whom we know from his own letters and the Lucan Paul, Vielhauer selects four themes: natural theology, the law, Christology, and eschatology. The conclusion he reaches is as follows:

> The author of Acts is in his Christology pre-Pauline, in his natural theology, concept of the law, and eschatology, post-Pauline. He presents no specifically Pauline idea. His "Paulinism" consists in his zeal for the worldwide Gentile mission and in his veneration for the greatest missionary to the Gentiles (p. 48).

It seems to me particularly important here to note, as Vielhauer does, though he, of course, is looking for contrasts, that in each of these four areas there is comparable material. For example, with Paul's speech at Athens in Acts 17 material in Romans 1 can be compared. This is not to say that Acts 17 and Romans 1 are identical in their teaching; they are not. The genuine, historical Paul writes:

> That which can be known of God is manifest among them, since God himself has manifested it to them. From the creation of the world onwards, the invisible attributes of God are plainly seen, since the mind can grasp them in the things that he has made. By his "invisible attributes" I mean his eternal power, his very Godhead (Rom. 1.19–20).

The connection, however, is quite different from that of the paragraph in Acts 17 which also draws attention to the action of God in creation:

> That which you worship in your ignorance I am declaring to you. . . . He made of one every race of men to dwell on all the face of the earth, he determined appointed seasons and the bounds of their habitation, that they should seek God, if by any means they might feel after him and find him; and indeed he is not far from each one of us . . . (Acts 17.23–7).

Acts is concerned with the education of mankind out of an ignorant worship into a full recognition of the God whom Paul preaches. The point of Paul's argument, on the other hand, is that all men are without excuse. Although they could have known God, they have in fact not treated him as God; they have not glorified him as God ought to be glorified, or given thanks to him. For this reason their senseless heart has been darkened, and they stand under God's wrath, which is revealed from heaven against all ungodliness and unrighteousness of men. So far from comforting men with the thought that nature has already taken them well on the way to grace, Paul shows that a potential but never actualized natural knowledge of God is man's condemnation.

With respect to law too there is (as Vielhauer shows) between Acts and Paul not only a difference but also a certain formal parallelism. In Acts 13.38f the Lucan Paul speaks superficially like the historical Paul. The law is a heavy burden, and does not suffice for justification; it is therefore senseless to require Gentiles to keep the law, which has notoriously failed to justify those who first received it. All this is said in something like the Pauline manner, but it has the appearance rather than the substance of Paulinism. Vielhauer says rightly that Luke, unlike Paul, is never troubled by the question, Is the law sin? For Luke, the law is certainly not sin; it is fairly good, though not so good as the gospel. For Paul, the law is at the same time the good word and the good gift of God, holy, righteous, good, given by the Holy Spirit, and the source of the sinful passions which work in our members, the source and cause not of life but of death. Thus Christ is the end of the law with a view to righteousness (Rom. 10.4); to seek justification through the law is not merely to seek in vain, it is to be separated from Christ, to have fallen from grace.

Time unfortunately does not permit me to give an account of Vielhauer's discussion of the Pauline and Lucan forms of Christology and eschatology. A somewhat similar overall presentation of the matter is given by E. Haenchen.[1] The first main question that he deals with is the problem of the law-free Gentile mission. Luke as well as Paul had to provide a basis and justification for this mission. Paul was able to do this from within, by his theological account of the purpose and significance of the law, which, in his view, rendered service to God, negative service perhaps, by shutting up all men in unbelief. Christ, however, proved to be the end of the law, achieving righteousness and freedom. "Of this view of the law, with its Yes and No in one, there is no trace in Acts" (p. 100). Luke, on the other hand, is not able to establish the right to exist of the Gentile mssion "from within, as Paul

[1] *Die Apostelgeschichte*, Kritisch-Exegetischer Kommentar über das Neue Testament (Göttingen 1965), pp. 99–103.

does. For this reason he must look for a means of establishing it from without" (p. 100). This foundation he finds in the miracles performed by the apostles. "The miracles provide the Gentile mission with the quiet conscience that is able to say, 'This is God's will'" (p. 100).

In Haenchen's treatment of the question there follow three features in which the Lucan picture of Paul is said to differ from that of the Pauline epistles.

(a) Luke describes Paul as a great miracle-worker; this (notwithstanding 2 Cor. 12.12) he was not.

(b) The Lucan Paul was an impressive orator; this too the historical Paul was not.

(c) For Luke there were only twelve apostles, of whom Paul was not one; but Paul believed that he was an apostle, and that in the highest sense.

Finally Haenchen deals with the relation between Jews and Christians. In Acts (he says), it is only the Christian preaching of the resurrection that inflames the opposition of the Jews against the Christians. "According to Acts, it is no peculiarly Pauline doctrine that brings Jewish persecution upon Paul" (p. 102). In fact, Luke represents Paul as an orthodox Pharisee. This representation, however, is unhistorical, and was designed as apologetic directed to the Roman authorities. Luke wished to show that the Christian message agreed with all that was best in the Jewish religion, and that the Christians might therefore claim the same measure of toleration which the Romans already showed to the Jews.

Vielhauer and Haenchen deal with the relation between Acts and Paul in general terms; it is regrettable that time does not permit me to discuss also essays that have dealt with particular details. Later I hope to come to a few critical observations; for the present, I must be content simply to mention a very different viewpoint. U. Wilckens, in the *Festschrift* for Paul Schubert,[1] writes under the title, "Interpreting Luke–Acts in a Period of Existential Theology". He denies that Luke corrupted Paul's theology. This is not to say, however, that the Lucan and Pauline theologies are identical. This they could not be, since the two authors wrote in two distinct historical situations.

[1] See note 2 on p. 87.

Paul had no possibility at all of making the history of Jesus the dominating center of his theology. By the same token, Luke could not possibly have built upon Pauline theology since his foundation was firmly laid out for him in the Jesus-tradition. Besides, the two men stood at different points in the history of the church: Luke knew neither Judaism nor Gnosticism from personal experience . . . we must simply not expect theological agreement between Luke and Paul (p. 68).

Nevertheless, the Pauline theology is not to be understood existentialistically, but in terms of *Heilsgeschichte*. This follows from the fact that Paul retains the framework of Jewish eschatology, affirming, for example, that the lapse of time brings salvation nearer (Rom. 13.11). This is *Heilsgeschichte*, not existentialism. Wilckens concludes his essay with the words:

It is Paul, interpreted existentially, who is so sharply set against Luke as the great but dangerous corrupter of the Pauline gospel. But the existentially interpreted Paul is not the historical Paul. And the essential points of theological criticism leveled against Luke are gained not so much from early Christian tradition itself as from the motifs of a certain modern school of theology which disregards or misinterprets essential aspects of early Christian thought. Recognition of these errors may well enliven the discussion of Luke's theology; for Luke, thus freed, is given the possibility of greatly stimulating our own thinking without compelling us to choose between himself and Paul (p. 77).

I must not, at this point, digress in order to discuss the right lines on which to interpret Pauline theology. It is, however, clear that, just as Vielhauer sees contacts and analogies, so Wilckens grants the existence, however caused and however explained, of a real difference between Pauline and Lucan theology. The effect of this is to sharpen the question whether the difference, the existence of which cannot be and is not denied, constitutes a corruption of Pauline theology, or is no more than a development and application of it to a new historical situation. This is the real problem of the Paulinism of Acts.

How can a satisfactory solution of this problem be achieved? The most important facts and observations are the following.

1. Luke was a Paulinist; that is, he admired Paul, perhaps defended him;[1] he imitated his theology, and (so far as he understood it) reproduced it. That Luke even considered depreciating the missionary, the account of whose work fills half his book, is incredible and impossible. Luke's position with regard to Paul is almost identical with that of his near contemporaries, Clement of Rome and Ignatius of Antioch. Clement writes:

> Let us take the noble examples of our own generation. On account of jealousy and envy the greatest and most righteous Pillars were persecuted, and contended even unto death. Let us set before our eyes the good apostles: Peter, who on account of unrighteous jealousy endured not one or two but many labours, and so, having borne testimony, went to his due place of glory. On account of jealousy and strife Paul pointed out the way to win the prize of patient endurance. He was seven times imprisoned, he was exiled, he was stoned, he acted as a herald in the East and in the West, and received the noble renown of his faith, having taught righteousness to the whole world and come to the bounds of the West; and when he had borne witness before rulers, so he departed from the world and went into the holy place, and became a supreme example of endurance (1 Clement 5).

We must observe here, without going into details, that Clement possessed a tradition about Paul similar to that contained in Acts: Paul engaged in wide-ranging missionary journeys, and was a famous preacher of the gospel, who suffered for his faith. It is also, however, to be noted that Clement, though he had read several Pauline letters, applies the word "pillar" to Peter and Paul, and not (as in Gal. 2.9) to James, Peter, and John, and certainly misunderstood so central a Pauline concept as righteousness.[2]

The most important passage in Ignatius is *Ephesians* 12.2:[3]

> The road of those who, by being killed, are to attain to God passes by you. You are fellow-initiates with Paul, who was

---

[1] As the author of the Pastorals appears to have done; see the reference in note 3 on p. 81 above. It is in this sense that Acts may be thought of as an "apology"; it is addressed not to Roman magistrates but to the Church.

[2] Grace, faith, election are other themes that sound in 1 Clement more Pauline than they are.

[3] See also *Romans* 4.3.

sanctified, who obtained a good report, who is worthy of felicitation, in whose footsteps may I be found when I attain to God, who in every letter makes mention of you in Christ Jesus.

Thus Ignatius too knows Paul as a travelling preacher, who suffered for his faith, and wrote letters; but, like Clement, though he knew Pauline letters and himself wrote formally similar letters, he had by no means fully understood the theological content of Paul's.[1] Clement and Ignatius both honoured Paul, and could think of themselves as his followers and imitators; in part they use his theological terminology; but into the depths of the theology itself they had not entered.

At least in this sense Luke too was a Paulinist. His narrative shows that it was Paul who brought the gospel, and the effect of Christ's work, to the ends of the earth. Luke shows him as being to the Jews a Jew, proving out of their Scriptures that Jesus was the Messiah (for example, 18.28); equally as a Greek to the Greeks, able, for example, in the Athens speech to quote one of their own poets (17.28). Luke knows that the great theme of Pauline theology is justification by faith, and this is duly introduced into another of the speeches:

Let it be known to you, brothers, that through this man forgiveness of sins is proclaimed to you, and in him every one who believes is justified from[2] all the things from which you could not be justified by the law of Moses (13.38–9).

The death of Paul is not narrated in Acts, but it is clearly predicted (for example, 21.10–14), and at 20.24 Paul says

I count my life of no value to myself, so that I may complete my course and the ministry which I received from the Lord Jesus, to testify the Gospel of the grace of God.

With these and similar words Luke prepares his readers for the martyrdom which he does not describe, though he evidently thought of it as the crown of Paul's career. One would draw the conclusion that Luke rated Paul higher than Peter, were it not

[1] For example, after speaking of Abraham and citing Gen. 15.6 as Paul does, Clement goes on to speak of Abraham's faith and hospitality on equal terms (10.6f; cf. 31.2).
[2] "To be justified from" ($\delta\iota\kappa\alpha\iota\omega\theta\hat{\eta}\nu\alpha\iota\ \dot{\alpha}\pi\acute{o}$) is not a characteristically Pauline phrase; see however Rom. 6.7.

that (except in 14.4,14) Paul is never in Acts described as an apostle.

2. A striking indication of the Paulinism of Acts lies in the fact that Luke not only mentions the conversion of Paul; he narrates it three times, once in straightforward reporting, twice in quotation from Paul himself. The three accounts are not identical. In Acts 9 Paul is journeying to Damascus with the intention of persecuting Christians. A light from heaven shines about him, he falls to the ground, and hears a voice saying to him, "Saul, Saul, why are you persecuting me?" He answers, "Who are you, Lord?" and learns that the speaker is Jesus. He travels on to Damascus, where he stays three days. At the end of this period, instructed by a vision, Ananias appears to heal Paul of his blindness, and Paul is baptized, presumably by Ananias, though this is not stated.

In Acts 22 the narrative, given in the course of Paul's speech in Jerusalem, is similar. The conversion takes place on a journey to Damascus undertaken for the purpose of continuing persecution. The conversation between the Lord and Paul is slightly expanded, but essentially unchanged. Ananias, now described as a "pious man according to the law", plays a larger part, in that he says to Paul, "You shall be a witness for him before all men of that which you have seen and heard"—that is, Paul's apostolic commission is incorporated in the narrative of the conversion. The account in Acts 26 (in the speech before Agrippa) is somewhat compressed, though the introductory question is longer: "Saul, Saul, why are you persecuting me? It is hard for you to kick against the goad." Ananias is not mentioned, and the Lord himself commissions Paul: "I have appeared to you for this purpose, namely, to appoint you as a servant and as a witness of what you have seen and of what will be shown you. And I will deliver you from the People and from the Gentiles, to whom I now send you, to open their eyes, that they may turn from darkness to light and from the power of Satan to God, that they may receive forgiveness of their sins and an inheritance among the sanctified through faith in me."

There are other small variations, which are familiar to every reader of Acts. The reader asks: How much did Jesus say to Paul? Who heard his words—Paul alone, or also his fellow-travellers? When was Paul commissioned to his apostolic task—

at the time of his conversion, or later? What role did Ananias play? These questions cannot be given precise answers. Conzelmann[1] has written:

> In the main, the three versions agree, but in detail they show variations, and indeed contradictions. Does this mean that Luke uses different sources? . . . No. The repetition is a stylistic device, . . . and the differences are to be explained as literary variation, and in part as negligence; they are connected with Luke's accommodation of his material to each particular situation (p. 59).

Conzelmann is right, and his observation is particularly important for the relation between Luke and Paul. There is no point in inquiring why Luke is not in complete agreement with the Pauline letters, for he is not in agreement with himself. The conversion narrative is a good example of Luke's way of writing; he prefers variation to literal accuracy. We therefore cannot expect to find literal agreement between Luke and Paul, and it is consequently impossible to use the narrative of Acts to correct, or even to check, the data of the epistles.[2] It must be assumed that, over against Acts, Paul is always right in the details that concern himself. Lucan variations at this level are not necessarily important; they may sometimes point to variant theological convictions on Luke's part, but equally and perhaps more often they may bear witness to nothing more than his love of variety. More important, in the study of parallels between Acts and Paul, is an investigation into the meaning and motivation of the narratives.

A good example is to be found in the story of Paul's flight from Damascus. In Acts, this event takes place shortly after the conversion (9.23ff). The Jews who live in Damascus determine to murder Paul, and watch the city gates day and night. Paul succeeds in escaping them, when the disciples let him down in a basket by the wall. A similar escape is described in 2 Corinthians 11.32f. In Damascus Paul is threatened by the Ethnarch of Aretas, king of the Nabataean Arabs, and escapes from him by the same method. We can hardly suppose that Paul made a habit of leaving cities in baskets; clearly we are dealing in Acts and 2 Corinthians

[1] H. Conzelmann, *Die Apostelgeschichte*, Handbuch zum Neuen Testament 7 (Tübingen 1963).
[2] For this theme see J. C. Hurd, *The Origin of 1 Corinthians* (1965), pp. 3–42.

with different accounts of the same event. The following points are to be noted.

(*a*) In broad outline Luke gives a correct picture: an attack is made upon Paul; his life is threatened, but he escapes, and in a basket. So far—and these are the essential points—Luke is right.

(*b*) Luke is nevertheless mistaken in important points. The enemy whom Paul had to fear was the Arab Ethnarch. Luke blamed the Jews, partly because he believed that the Jews were always inimical to the Christians, and that if anyone threatened an apostle the odds were that the assailant was a Jew.

(*c*) Between the two narratives there is a noteworthy difference in motivation. The context of 2 Corinthians 11 shows plainly that for Paul the event was an outstanding example of the humiliation which he was obliged to endure in the service of the gospel. "Who is weak, and I am not weak? Who is offended, and I do not burn? If I have to boast, then I will boast of my weakness" (11.29f). The atmosphere in Acts is quite different. This event is the first example of the rule (as one might almost call it) that in all circumstances Paul always emerges as the victor. This is exemplified repeatedly. His adversary in Cyprus, Elymas or Bar-Jesus, is blinded. In Lystra Paul is stoned, but quickly stands up again and goes into the city. In Philippi he is arrested and imprisoned, but is set free by an earthquake. He sufferers shipwreck, but escapes safely to land. In Rome he is able to proclaim the kingdom of God and to teach about the Lord Jesus Christ in all freedom, unhindered. Paul is the great hero of the Christian mission, who always acts under divine guidance and protection, and, as I have said, the Damascus episode is the first example of this. Behind this presentation of Paul's personal adventures lies a conviction which Luke held not only in personal terms. For him (as for the author of the Pastorals—2 Tim. 2.9) it is the word of God that is not bound. This is shown by the fact that, as we have seen, Luke was aware of Paul's approaching martyrdom, and also by the narrative in Acts 15, where Luke shows that the Pauline gospel, free from the Law and free for all men, is the true victor, whose progress no one can halt. But it is Luke's characteristic method to express this fundamentally theological conviction through stories about the

great missionary, and especially through his triumphs and
escapes.

3. When these characteristic methods of Luke's are borne in
mind, it is the more surprising that his account of Paul's conversion is so Pauline. Luke, though writing biographical history,
makes no attempt to provide the event with a psychologizing
explanation. The heavenly light and voice are indeed familiar
features of theophanies, and Luke uses them and the conversation
between Jesus and Paul to make the story livelier and more impressive. But the chief element in his version of the story is the meeting
between Jesus and Paul; and so it is also for Paul himself. Here
too, however, a distinction is to be made. For Paul, this meeting
is the last of the resurrection appearances (1 Cor. 15.8); in Acts,
this is something that it cannot be, since according to Luke it has
been preceded by the ascension, an event unknown (as an incident,
capable of narration) to Paul. Luke avoids the difficulty by
making no attempt to explain how the ascended Christ could
appear to Paul, and in any case the similarity is far greater than the
difference. The Lucan Paul also could say

> It pleased him who separated me from my mother's womb and
> called me through his grace to reveal his Son to me, that I
> might preach him among the Gentiles (Gal. 1.15f),

though Luke could certainly not have added the next words,

> Immediately I did not consult with flesh and blood, nor did I
> go up to Jerusalem, to those who were apostles before me.

For Luke it was important to keep Paul as close as possible to the
primitive apostles, and in Acts Paul soon travels to Jerusalem
(9.26).

4. Luke rightly saw that Paul's conversion was essentially an
encounter between Paul and the risen Jesus; but from this fact
he failed to draw the right conclusions. He did not even recognize
that Paul had drawn these conclusions. Paul himself summed
them up succinctly in Philippians:

> The things that once were credits to me I have reckoned for
> Christ's sake as loss. Yes, indeed, and I count all things to be
> loss for the sake of the surpassing worth of the knowledge of

Christ Jesus my Lord, for whose sake I have counted all things loss, and esteem them as dung, that I may gain Christ, and be found in him, not having my righteousness, the righteousness that comes from the law, but that which comes through faith in Christ, the righteousness that comes from God on the basis of faith (3.7–9).

This complete revaluation of the presuppositions of his entire life meant in particular a revaluation and a new understanding of the law and of Jewish eschatology.[1] The law, which had cursed Jesus as one hanged upon a tree (Gal. 3.13, quoting Deut. 21.23), could no longer determine the relations between God and mankind. Scripture had shut up all men and all things under sin. The legal way to God, which had proved impracticable, was no longer open even as a theoretical possibility; but, over against this old way, God had now brought forward the eschatological programme. Final redemption was already at hand in the crucified Christ; thus Christ was at the same time the end of the law, and an anticipation of the end of history. That Luke did not see, or at any rate failed to express, all this, is the most important example of that superficiality of which I wrote in the previous chapter.

There are two examples of this superficiality which I do not need to mention at this point. One is the question of apostleship, which I dealt with in the previous chapter; the other is the Gentile mission, which I shall refer to in the next. At present, I wish to mention, in a brief summary, two further themes.

1. The first is Gnosis. It seems to me beyond dispute that no direct discussion of gnosis and the gnostic problem of primitive Christianity is to be found in Acts. Even in the account of the Samaritan Simon (8.9–24) there is no hint that Simon was (as later generations believed him to have been) the first gnostic heretic. It is Simon's bad ethical behaviour—his simony—not his bad theology of which Luke complains. This, however, does not mean that Luke was unaware of a gnostic problem. Acts 20.29 (Paul knows that after his death grievous wolves will enter the Church, not sparing the flock) shows that Luke was well aware that false doctrine would in due course arise in the Church, but

---

[1] I have made these points more fully in *The Epistle to the Romans* (1957), pp. 7ff.

he represents the origin of heresy as post-Pauline. In the whole of the speech to the Ephesians elders there is no hint that heresy had already made its presence felt; it was a future peril. This picture is certainly unhistorical. Gnostic and other false doctrines were already common in the Pauline period; but Luke was concerned to depict this as a golden age of peace and sound teaching. His unhistorical picture owes its origin to the method Luke used in combating the errors of his own day. He points his contemporaries back to the good old days of the apostles; but there was no point in doing this if the old days could not be shown to have been also good. The method was in a sense sound; it was right to refer the Church to its origins; but Luke understood it to mean that he must represent the Church of the early years as relatively free from spot, wrinkle, or blemish—relatively free, for incidents such as that of Ananias and Sapphira (5.1–11) are the sort of exception that proves the rule. It was from the example of the earliest Church that the Church of his own day must learn how Christians live and what they preach; what Luke apparently did not see was that its conflicts might have been even more instructive than its example.

2. The second theme to receive brief reference here can be regarded as a generalization of the first; it is the question of Lucan *Frühkatholizismus* ("primitive catholicism"—but neither this nor any other English translation is entirely satisfactory, and it may be best to let the German stand). On this subject the most diverse opinions have been expressed, and it is particularly important to define the term *Frühkatholizismus* as accurately as possible. It is sometimes so loosely used that it can be taken to denote anything that belongs to the second or third Christian generation. In this case Acts certainly bears the marks of *Frühkatholizismus*. It was inevitable that some of the earliest forms of eschatological expectation, the hope, for example, that the coming of Christ from heaven would take place within the first generation of Christians, should disappear, not on account of theological presuppositions but simply through the lapse of time. It became simply impossible to believe that the whole process of redemption would work itself out within one generation, though naturally it was still possible, and continued to be believed, that the end would come very soon. In addition, at a time when the gnostic move-

ment was in full course it was inevitable that there should be some kind of reaction to it. Thus merely to say that a book written about the end of the century manifests a transformed eschatology and a reaction to gnosis, is to say nothing at all. The word *Frühkatholizismus* must be more precisely and narrowly delimited, and be related not to any but to a specific kind of reaction to the eschatological and gnostic problems. If we bear in mind the later development of catholicism in the second century, it seems clear that this special kind of reaction must be seen as a growing concern for the form of the Church—not simply for its good order but for a particular structure; for orthodoxy—not only for a pure preaching of the gospel but for a right formulation of faith; and for the sacraments. When *Frühkatholizismus* is so defined, it must be admitted that it is not so easy to find it in Acts. But to this question, and to the related but perhaps even more fundamental question, whether Luke corrupted or merely applied Pauline theology, I shall return in the next chapter.

7

The Acts and the Origins
of Christianity

In the previous two chapters I used an approach to the problems of Acts which lay primarily in the fields of history and of theology. I asked, for example, What sort of picture of the apostles do we gain from Acts? How does this compare with the picture of the apostle Paul which Paul himself gives us? How in general is Acts related to the Pauline letters, and to the form of theological thinking we call Paulinism? That is to say, we have so far attempted to bring out the special characteristics of Acts by means of historical and theological comparisons. For this purpose it was necessary to have an historical and theological norm, and this norm we found in the person of Paul. There is in fact no other. This lack of other comparisons is the less to be regretted because the Pauline epistles provide invaluable glimpses of the history of the first Christian generation, and Pauline theology is the heart of New Testament theology as a whole. In this chapter I am not abandoning the comparative method of my previous two chapters; in the study of Acts it is unavoidable and indispensable, whether it is used alone or in combination with other methods; I should like, however, to include literary questions and literary methods in the discussion. Historical and theological comparisons cannot be carried out without a certain amount of guesswork and conjecture, and there is only one method of evaluating the tendencies of an author that can claim the virtue of objectivity. One must observe how the author uses his sources: alterations, additions, omissions—these will show, as nothing else can do, the writer's interests, even though (as we have seen) these may sometimes amount to no more than an interest in literary variation. Even this kind of interest, however, is not unimportant; it plays its part, for example, in the comparison of the Third Gospel with Matthew and Mark which is the primary means of bringing out the peculiar character of this Gospel. When we turn from the Gospels to Acts, however, the problem is, Where do we find the appropriate material for comparison? The plain answer to this question is that there is no such material;[1] there are, however, two kinds of literary comparisons that it is possible and useful to make.

1. The first is in the field of textual criticism. The whole problem of the text of Acts cannot be discussed or even adequately raised in this study. Every student of Acts knows that, broadly speaking, the textual witnesses fall into two groups, which present two types of text. On the one hand, there is the Egyptian, or Old Uncial, Text, found notably in the great uncials Codex Vaticanus (B), Codex Sinaiticus (א), and so on. On the other hand, there is in Codex Bezae (D), the Latin versions, and a number of other authorities, the so-called Western Text. It is now widely recognized that it is impossible to embrace one of these texts as "right" and to reject the other as "wrong". Textual criticism is not so easy as that, and no textual type is absolutely right or absolutely wrong. In every variant each group must be considered without prejudice, and it may prove that now one, now the other, is to be followed. It is nevertheless true that each type has its characteristics, and it is possible and rewarding to compare them. Comparisons of this kind have more than once been made, and I propose next to consider two recent attempts to define the Western Text over against the Old Uncial.

The first comparison is that of P. H. Menoud.[2] After a detailed discussion of a number of variants he sums up his findings in four paragraphs.

(a) *Jews and Christians* The Western Text manifests an anti-Jewish tendency; it brings out the fact that the Jews are responsible for the death of Jesus and for the sufferings of the apostles; even so, they are powerless to prevent the founding of the Church and the spread of its message. For example, at Acts 4.14 according to B the Jews could say nothing against

---

[1] Attempts have been made to show that Luke knew and used Paul's letters, but they are not convincing.

[2] "The Western Text and the Theology of Acts", in *Bulletin* II of *Studiorum Novi Testamenti Societas* (1951), pp. 19–32.

the apostles; according to D neither could they do anything against them.

(b) *The Apostles and the Church*   The Western Text is more universalist than the Old Uncial. For example, the effect of the alterations made by the Western Text in the Old Testament quotation in Acts 2.17ff is to make Peter a preacher of the Pauline universalist gospel. It would almost be true to say that in the Western Text the importance of Paul is minimized—almost, but not quite. Thus "the emphasis in the D reading in Acts xv.2 is not against Paul but in favour of the authority and unity of the church" (p. 29).

(c) *The Holy Spirit*   The Western Text has no special theology of the Holy Spirit, but a heightened interest in the subject. The Spirit is mentioned more frequently, and with the full title. The Western editor is interested in gifts of the Spirit, but his tendency cannot be dismissed as Montanist, for he ascribes no special place to women, as the Montanists did.

(d) *The Lord Jesus Christ*   Here too the Western Text prefers the full title, sometimes expanding the simple name Jesus.

A similar but more detailed attempt to characterize the Western Text, or at least its most important representative, is made by E. J. Epp in his book, *The Theological Tendency of Codex Bezae Cantabrigiensis in Acts*.[1] The conclusion of this careful study is that the tendency of D (and this comes very near to saying, the tendency of the Western Text) is anti-Jewish. This anti-Jewishness is expressed in three ways; the threefold analysis brings Epp nearer to Menoud than he appears at first sight to be.

(a) In comparison with what appears in other texts the Jews are represented as more inimical to Jesus, and their guilt is underlined by increased emphasis on the Lordship and Messiahship of Jesus—it is not simply Jesus, but the *Lord* Jesus *Christ* whom they reject.

(b) The Jews do not accept the gospel so readily as the Gentiles do, and make a smaller contribution to the Christian faith and the Christian Church; correspondingly the role of the Gentiles is exalted in D.

[1] *Society for New Testament Studies, Monograph Series 3* (1966).

(*c*) The leading Jews appear to be more violently opposed to the apostles; correspondingly the apostles stand out more plainly as the leaders of the Church.

Occasionally Epp draws attention to other tendencies; he notes, for example, an emphasis upon the Holy Spirit, upon faith, upon penitence, upon preaching. These tendencies, however, are not so important as anti-Jewishness.

These descriptions of the Western Text which we owe to Menoud and Epp are in general convincing; it may, however, be said that they miss the main point, for in fact the chief tendency of the Western Text is simply to exaggerate. The editor does not so much introduce new tendencies into Acts as make clearer and more emphatic tendencies that were already there.[1] In all manuscripts and texts of Acts one can see anti-Jewishness, an emphasis on the leadership and the preaching of the apostles, an interest in the Holy Spirit, and so on. These tendencies are underlined in the Western Text.[2] We ought, however, to be grateful to the Western editor (and to the modern writers who have so clearly exposed his work), for he has brought out important features of Acts. The brighter colours of the Western Text make the outlines of the book clearer and easier to understand. They also indicate which features of Acts were still alive and impressive in the second century, when the characteristics of the Western Text developed. These, however, as we have seen, are on the whole simply the main features of Acts as the book was originally planned, and from this we are able to deduce that Acts belongs to the second-century development of Christianity, though indeed in its original form to a very early stage in that development. This observation we shall have to keep in mind; it may facilitate the next step in our review. The roots of Acts are to be found in the age of the Pauline letters; its branches spread out into the world of the second century. Clearly to grasp these two points will contribute to a precise understanding of Acts.

[1] The form of this sentence assumes what I believe to be true, though I cannot support it here—that the Western Text, though it contains some very old features, is a second-century edition of Acts. The argument in the text could be restated in terms of other views.

[2] W. L. Knox once said to me, "The Western Editor reminds me of a not very intelligent Sunday School teacher, trying to make the Bible stories more interesting for the children."

2. We may now proceed to the second kind of literary comparison, which can, with some reserve, be applied to Acts. It is natural to turn from textual criticism to source criticism. But what are the sources of Acts? In the Third Gospel we can make use of the parallel columns of a Synopsis, and the opening verses of the book correspond to this fact:

> Since many have taken in hand to draw up a narrative concerning the events that have taken place among us . . . it seemed good to me also to write . . . (Luke 1.1–4).

In writing his Gospel Luke could draw not only upon eye-witnesses and ministers of the word but also upon written sources. It was not so, or at least we have no positive evidence that it was so, with the writing of Acts. We know no parallel narratives, and Luke appeals to none. So far as we can tell, he did not know even the Pauline letters which we have in the New Testament.

Nevertheless, the source criticism of Acts has been practised for a long time, so that its history can be no more than hinted here; for details I may refer to the excellent book by J. Dupont.[1] The most notable name of an earlier epoch is Harnack,[2] who in Acts 2–5 observed doublets and contradictions, which led him to deduce in these chapters the existence of two sources, Jerusalem A (3.1—5.16) and Jerusalem B (2.1–47; 5.17–42), and saw in 6.1—8.4; 11.19–30; 13.1—15.35 an Antiochene source, in which the development of events was regarded and narrated from the point of view of Antioch. All this can be described as "classical literary criticism", after the familiar manner of the Pentateuchal criticism of Graf and Wellhausen. Harnack's theories were examined in a notable article by J. Jeremias,[3] who made the two Jerusalem sources seem very improbable, and was willing to recognize the Antiochene as the only written source behind Acts 1—15. He defined this source somewhat differently, as follows: 6.1—8.4; 9.1–30; 11.19–30; 12.25—14.28; 15.35ff. From this analysis Jeremias concluded that the so-called First Missionary Journey took place after the Apostolic Council. In more recent years the source criticism of Acts has moved into a wider field,

---

[1] *The Sources of Acts* (1964).
[2] See especially *The Acts of the Apostles* (1909).
[3] "Untersuchungen zum Quellenproblem der Apostelgeschichte", in *Zeitschrift für die neutestamentliche Wissenschaft* 36 (1937), pp. 205–21.

H

in that it has come to be recognized that in the composition of the book written sources, oral tradition, and redaction have all played their different parts. A general statement of this kind does not end the matter; it gives it a new turn, and it remains to be asked not only what the sources were and where they originated, but how written sources, oral sources, and redaction are related to one another. This question may be illustrated by a well-known dispute between Haenchen and Bultmann.

In his Commentary[1] Haenchen emphasized the independent, creative work of Luke. Luke (in his view) was not an historian, who weighed his sources and carefully worked them together. On the basis of a theologically conceived idea of the significance of the history of the primitive Church he freely made up (*gedichtet*) this history. That does not mean (according to Haenchen) that the whole story is free invention; it does mean, however, that when studying a paragraph of Acts one ought first to inquire about the author's purpose rather than about his sources. Over against this position Bultmann puts two questions, which he states as follows.[2]

(1) Is the analysis, which works reciprocally with the interpretation of the basic meaning, always kept firmly in view? Is it not often subordinated to the inquiry into the basic meaning of the whole, so that the latter is actually taken as a valid criterion against the use of a source?

(2) Does not Haenchen treat the question of written sources too lightly? Does he not too often content himself with the simple remark that, here or there, there is present a "tradition", without asking more precisely what kind of tradition it is?

Bultmann is certainly right in this, that it would be possible to grasp Luke's theological presuppositions with much greater exactness if one could suppose that he used not an undefined "tradition" but a written source, into which he interpolated his own words and sentences. But this observation, true as it is, cannot prove that Luke did in fact have such a written source at his disposal. Haenchen replied to the questions posed by

---

[1] See above, p. 89, n. 1; pp. 72–80, 93–9, 671–5.
[2] "Zur Frage nach den Quellen der Apostelgeschichte", in *New Testament Essays: Studies in Memory of T. W. Manson*, ed. A. J. B. Higgins (1959), pp. 70f.

Bultmann in his article in the *Festschrift* for Jeremias.[1] Bultmann's position, he said, was an over-simplification.

It looks as if we have here a simple solution: Take the earlier source analysis, and connect it directly with the analysis of composition. This means that one would have to suppose that the New Testament author had written out his sources (enriched with his own additions) and put them together so cleverly that they produced the picture to which he was himself inclined. Both would then be right: the source critic of that brilliant period, which can be denoted by such names as Harnack, Wellhausen, Schwartz, and Bousset, and the new method of treatment, with which in Acts Martin Dibelius made so promising a beginning.

But we cannot treat the matter as simply as that (p. 155).

Haenchen continues with a discussion of the narrative of Acts 15; we cannot follow him into the details here. The moral of the dispute between the champion of written sources and the composition analyst seems, however, to be clear: the one fundamental error in this kind of study, not least as applied to Acts, is to neglect any possibly relevant method. None may be excluded *a priori*. In each passage one must consider the possibility that Luke may have used a written source or sources, and interpolated his own redactional glosses; equally, in each passage one must consider the possibility that oral traditions have been worked over, or that Luke has constructed a narrative on the basis of his general view of the situation and course of development. These possibilities are capable of combination in a variety of ways, and throughout the hand of the author may be perceived, as he seeks out material of every sort and reduces it to a connected unity. In this way it can be seen that Luke's historical writing was determined partly by the materials that were available to him, and partly by the historical and theological convictions and presuppositions that he brought to his work. It is precisely at this point that the value of our comparison between Acts and Paul appears, for by means of it we acquire a measuring-rod which is indispensable for the analysis of Luke's narrative material—and that not only where there is

---

[1] "Quellenanalyse und Kompositionsanalyse in Act 15", in *Judentum, Urchristentum, Kirche, Festschrift für Joachim Jeremias*, ed. W. Eltester (Berlin 1960).

parallel narrative in, or immediately behind, the Pauline letters.

In this short study it is unfortunately impossible to analyse in detail even one section of Acts. I propose, however, by way of example to examine briefly the account of Stephen and the Seven (Acts 6, 7). It is characteristic of Luke's narrative style that this story, when read through quickly, gives the impression of unity and coherence. Within the primitive Church a need arises: the Hellenist widows are being overlooked in the daily administration of alms. The apostles, as leaders of the community, appoint seven of its members to care for the widows and ensure a proper distribution of supplies, while they themselves attend to prayer and the ministry of the word. One of the Seven, Stephen, shows himself to be an outstanding evangelist and controversialist; as such he provokes the Jews, and brings their wrath upon himself. They arrest him, and bring him before the Council; in spite of his energetic speech in his own defence he is condemned to death and executed. A simple and satisfactory story—or is it?

In fact, when the story is read again more slowly and carefully, it seems anything but simple and satisfactory. The following are the most important of the problems it raises.

1. The Seven, Stephen and his colleagues, do not carry out the task for which they are appointed. After Acts 6.3 we do not hear another word about the unfortunate Hellenist widows. About the Seven we have a few historical reminiscences, but they are of a quite different kind. The relatively detailed account of the life and death of Stephen (who can hardly have had time to feed the hungry widows) follows at once (6.8—8.3). Philip carries out a mission in Samaria (8.5–25), converts the Ethiopian (8.26–40), and later appears in Caesarea, bearing the title εὐαγγελιστής (21.8). All this is well known; less frequently recognized perhaps is the fact that the Seven were not in a position to carry out the task for which Acts says they were appointed. This task arose out of a γογγυσμός (6.1), a complaint; that is, the earlier administration of the Church's almsgiving had led to attention to the Hebrews ('Εβραῖοι) and neglect of the Hellenists, and thus to a measure of ill-feeling. This unsatisfactory consequence could have been removed only if two committees had been appointed, one to care for the Hebrews and one for the Hellenists, or if a joint Hebrew–Hellenist committee had been formed. The apostles, who might

reasonably have represented the Hebrews, explicitly refuse to undertake the work (6.2,4), and no Hebrew was appointed—as has often been observed, all seven names are of Hellenistic origin (6.5). The event which is described in 6.1 is in itself quite a possible one. Not every charitable administration does its work to the satisfaction of all, and racial and linguistic differences can give rise to serious problems—of all this we are well aware. But in Acts 6 and 7 there is no serious attempt to find a solution for problems of this kind. The separation between the Twelve and the Seven (supposing the two groups to be historical) must have taken place differently from the way in which Luke describes it, and on other grounds.

2. The attack on Stephen is in Luke's account unexplained—and yet appears at the same time to be in part at least justified (though this can hardly be the impression that Luke intended to give). Before the accusation is brought against him Stephen has only performed wonders and signs (τέρατα καὶ σημεῖα, 6.8). Jews of Cyrene, Alexandria, Cilicia, and Asia have disputed with him (6.9f); these were Hellenist Jews. They could not withstand the wisdom and the Spirit with which he spoke. Their accusation is given in two forms, in verse 11, and in verses 13 and 14. In verses 13f it is expressly ascribed to false witnesses; the same is suggested in verse 11 by the words ὑπέβαλον ἄνδρας. But, if we are to take the speech ascribed to Stephen himself as evidence, the accusation of verses 13f, whoever made it, was true, at least in part. Certainly Stephen does not speak against God, or indeed against Moses. He does not speak explicitly against the law, but he does speak against the Temple (the τόπος), which was prescribed by the law. If he said that Jesus would destroy the Temple, then this was not far from what is prophesied in the synoptic apocalypses (Mark 13.2 and parallels; cf. 14.58; 15.29); and according to the synoptic tradition Jesus did change the Mosaic customs (τὰ ἔθη ἃ παρέδωκεν ἡμῖν Μωϋσῆς)—for example, he changed quite radically the laws about clean and unclean foods (Mark 7.14–23). It is hardly credible that Luke had in his own mind a really clear picture of the accusation that brought about Stephen's death, although here and there glimpses of historical truth appear in his account. Probably the Seven were leading Hellenist Jews who became Christians and separated themselves from the Temple

and so brought upon themselves the anger of the Jerusalem population, and especially of the Temple administration. But this Luke does not say; it can only be inferred from the hints, and especially from the loose ends, of his story.

3. Stephen's speech, as we read it in the trial narrative of Acts 7, is no "speech for the defence". In itself, that observation does not prove that the speech cannot have been historical. We are familiar with the fact that an accused person, charged on religious or political grounds, will use the opportunity of his appearance in court to propagate his opinions, without strict regard for relevance. But this comment, true as it is, cannot adequately account for the long lecture on Old Testament history which is put into Stephen's mouth. The origin of the speech is a special problem to which I must not now digress. Possibly it belongs to the debates which took place between Christian and non-Christian Jews; in this case it would, interestingly enough, belong to the historical, though not to the Lucan origin of the Seven. But in no case does it belong to the trial scene.

4. A fourth question may be briefly mentioned in passing. It has often, and rightly, been noted[1] that parts of the narrative about Stephen describe legal proceedings carried out in a law court, others a popular lynching. It may be that Luke used and loosely combined two sources; it may be that his own mind was not clear. At all events, in this respect also his narrative raises questions that it does not answer.

5. As Harnack and others[2] have seen, Luke draws a line which leads from the appointment of the Seven to the conversion of the Gentiles.

> On that day there arose a great persecution against the church in Jerusalem. All were scattered through the districts of Judaea and Samaria except the apostles ($\pi\acute{a}\nu\tau\epsilon\varsigma$ $\delta\iota\epsilon\sigma\pi\acute{a}\rho\eta\sigma\alpha\nu$. . . $\pi\lambda\grave{\eta}\nu$ $\tau\hat{\omega}\nu$ $\dot{a}\pi o\sigma\tau\acute{o}\lambda\omega\nu$: 8.1).

> Those who had been scattered ($o\acute{\iota}$ $\delta\iota\alpha\sigma\pi\alpha\rho\acute{\epsilon}\nu\tau\epsilon\varsigma$) went about, preaching the word (8.4).

[1] So, for example, Lake and Cadbury in *Beginnings of Christianity* iv (1933), p. 84; cf. Haenchen, *Commentary*, p. 247.
[2] For example, Lake and Cadbury, op. cit., p. 127.

Those who had been scattered (οἱ διασπαρέντες) on account of the persecution that arose over Stephen went on as far as Phoenicia, Cyprus, and Antioch, speaking the word to no one but Jews. But there were some of them, men of Cyprus and Cyrene, who when they came to Antioch spoke also the Greeks (ἐλάλουν καὶ πρὸς τοὺς ῞Ελληνας, that is, Gentiles), preaching the Lord Jesus (11.19f).

These points trace out a straight line: the scattering of Stephen's Hellenist associates was the first step in the Gentile mission. But this was not so; the matter was far less simple. Perhaps (so, for example, Cadbury)[1] the first step is to be seen in the event of Pentecost (2.9ff). In Acts 8 we read an account of the conversion of the Ethiopian, who, as a eunuch cannot have been a full proselyte (Deut. 23.1(2)). In Acts 10.1—11.18 we have the long, detailed story of Cornelius and of his conversion by Peter, which Peter himself in 15.7 mentions as the beginning of the Gentile mission. In the absence of evidence, we can only guess what Paul was doing in Caesarea and Tarsus (9.30), but it is a natural guess that Barnabas brought him to Antioch because he knew that Paul had already taken part in Christian activity among Gentiles. Thus in another very important respect the story of Stephen does not agree with the total plan of Acts.

These are the most important difficulties that arise in the analysis of the narrative about Stephen and the Hellenists. There are several other points of detail which we cannot handle here, though they are not unimportant. That Acts 6 and 7 are a composition, and a Lucan composition, is a conclusion that can hardly be avoided. It is, however, equally clear that it is not a free composition. The speech is so long, and contains so many unessential details, that the reader can hardly doubt that it was taken from a written source. It is, however, also possible that this source stood in some relation to the actual origin of the Seven, since both had their setting within Hellenistic Judaism. It is probable that Luke, writing later in the century, no longer understood the origin and the original significance of the Seven, and improbable that he found the story of the Hellenist widows in a written source. More important are the results, as Luke narrates them, of the persecution connected with Stephen, and to understand these

[1] Cadbury, *Beginnings of Christianity* v (1933), pp. 67f.

we must look briefly at a second Acts narrative—the conversion of Cornelius.

In this story I shall draw attention to only two questions.

1. What is the relation between the vision, which Peter sees in Acts 10.9–16, and the account of his meeting with Cornelius? In the vision Peter sees all the animals of the world. The heavenly voice calls to him, Rise, Peter, kill and eat. It is already a problem that Peter hesitates to obey the command. All the creatures are there, clean as well as unclean; why does he assume that he is expected to kill and eat an unclean animal? His hesitation gives the heavenly Speaker the opportunity of instructing him further: he must not consider unclean what God (we should perhaps say, by implication) declares to be clean. If the narrative ended at this point, we should naturally conclude that it referred to the question (much discussed in early Christian circles) what foods a Christian was allowed to eat, what he must reject. But in 10.28, Peter, referring back to the vision, says, God has shown me that I ought to describe no man as common or unclean. To what then does the vision refer? to beasts, or (by allegory) to men? It is natural to jump to the conclusion that the vision narrative and the conversion narrative were drawn from two distinct sources, but this is a conclusion that should not be drawn too quickly—though in the end it may turn out to be true. The question about the cleanness or uncleanness of the Gentiles was closely bound up with the question about the cleanness or uncleanness of their food. It is not easy to decide whether Luke failed to see and understand the relation between two parts both originally belonging to the same story, or whether he unadvisedly put together two independent pieces. Peter never makes a clear statement of the logical connection: God has shown me that I may regard no food as unclean, therefore that I may eat all foods, therefore that I may have dealings and fellowship with all men, Gentiles as well as Jews, therefore that I may seek to win all men, Gentiles as well as Jews, for Christ. From the Pauline epistles, however, it appears that the question about foods did not become sharp till after the beginning of the mission, and from the Apostolic Decree of Acts 15.20,29 that the Christians in Jerusalem never accepted that the food laws had been completely abrogated. This state of things Luke at the end of the century could not understand, and this supports the view

that he received the account of the vision as a separate piece and incorporated it in the Cornelius story. If this is so, however, it is remarkable that he edited it so sparingly. Apart from the reference in 10.28 (and the corresponding reference in 11.5–10) the story of the vision has left no trace in the main narrative. This in turn suggests that the Cornelius story was originally an independent unity, not a Lucan composition. Whether the vision was taken out of tradition or simply created by Luke is disputed.[1] It seems to me more probable that it was taken out of the earlier tradition, because, as we have already seen, it does not correspond to the Apostolic Decree, which did not regard all foods (though it may have regarded all animals) as clean.

2. In Acts 11.3 the complaint is brought against Peter, You went in to uncircumcised people and ate with them. Peter answers the charge, and at the end of the paragraph (11.18) the Jewish Christians confess, Why then, to the Gentiles also God has given the repentance that leads to life. They do not demand that the Gentiles should be circumcised; on the contrary, any such event is excluded by the narrative. Later, however (Acts 15), the same question is taken up again, and receives a new answer; and Luke appears not to notice that he is repeating himself. Now it is to be noted that in 11.4–17 there is no fresh material. Luke simply reproduces the contents of the previous chapter with a few small but characteristic variations. Acts 11.1 is probably a Lucan connecting link; 11.2f a part of the source used in Acts 10; 11.4–17 repetitive summary; 11.18 the continuation of 11.2,3. This means that in 10.1–8, 17–24, 30–48; 11.2,3,18 we have (apart from a few small redactional glosses) a narrative source, whose theme was the founding of the mixed, Jewish–Gentile community in Caesarea, and its acceptance in Jerusalem.

The conclusion to be drawn from these observations is that the literary problem of the sources of Acts is very closely bound up with the problem, at once theological and historical, of the Gentile mission. For example, Luke combined the story of Stephen and the Seven with a narrative of the founding of the mixed Jewish–Gentile Church in Antioch, with the result that

[1] Conzelmann (above, p. 95, n. 1), for example, thinks the vision narrative traditional (p. 61), Haenchen (above, p. 89, n. 1) that Luke himself composed it (p. 307).

we can now see neither event quite clearly. In a similar way he combined an account of a vision granted to Peter, which originally was related to the question about foods, with the establishing of the mixed Jewish–Gentile Church in Caesarea; here too the result is that a new cycle of problems comes into being. From the Lucan point of view the stories are edifying and satisfactory; the historical critic can hardly estimate them in the same way.

A further result may be noted here. Sources in Acts are often bound up with particular persons and places. It has been asked, Can we conceive that a Church of the first century should keep archives and minute-books? In general, the answer to this question is certainly No. The Churches of the first century were awaiting the coming of the Lord, not preparing for the arrival of the historical critic. There is, however, one exception to this general principle. It is probable that a Church would preserve (by no means necessarily on paper) a recollection of its origin and of its founder. This account would necessarily represent a special form and a distinctive understanding of the conditions for the admission of Gentiles.

It is in this way that the literary problems, and especially the historical and theological obscurities, of Acts came into being. Though up to a point true, it is quite inadequate to say that in Acts we are looking at the personalities and events of the 30s, 40s, and 50s from a stand-point at the end of the century, as though the events of the earlier years were simple and self-explanatory. This they certainly were not. It was already a very complex and unclear picture that was further obscured by the fact that Luke saw it at long range, from the end of the century. To this confused picture Paul made important contributions; but that there were other contributions, both good and bad, is shown by the Pauline letters themselves.

At this point I return to an observation in Vielhauer's well-known essay on the Paulinism of Acts. I have already (p. 88 above) quoted these words: "The author of Acts is in his Christology pre-Pauline, in his natural theology, concept of the law, and eschatology, post-Pauline." The question immediately presents itself, What, in a sentence like this, can the words "pre-Pauline", "post-Pauline" mean? If we are to use chronological terms at all, must we not say that Luke's Christology too was post-Pauline, since he himself was post-Pauline? Vielhauer's point is of course clear enough: in the realm of Christology the post-Pauline Luke thought in the same way that some pre-Pauline Christians had done; but just so far as this is true it means that it is impossible to trace a chronological development in Christology, since the same Christology—Luke's—has to be designated both pre-Pauline and post-Pauline. This fact is worth noting, for it may serve as a signpost to point out the right way to handle the problem of *Frühkatholizismus* (pp. 99f above). It is impossible to arrange a simple order: (1) Primitive Church; (2) Paul; (3) Deuteropaulines; (4) *Frühkatholizismus*; (5) Developed catholicism. From the first Paul had to wrestle with the elements of truth and falsehood in *Frühkatholizismus*. We cannot find a Christian Golden Age in which these, or at least some of them, were not present.

Luke makes a somewhat artificial distinction between his own age, and what he conceives to be the good old days of his hero Paul. They were good old days, but not in the rather naive sense that Luke seems to have in mind. They were good, not because they were uniformly pure and peaceful, but because, though tumultuous and troubled, they were creative; and Paul was a creative theologian not in spite of his conflicts but because of them. The distinction Luke makes complicates the relation between his theology and Paul's. It can be confidently affirmed that Luke had no intention of corrupting or perverting Paul's theology; he intended to apply it, but, as we have seen, he made the application without Paul's critical theological insight. What this means is that though Luke himself is not a representative of *Frühkatholizismus*, in the sense that Clement and Ignatius are, he nevertheless made a contribution to the development of *Frühkatholizismus*. In other words, we must not take Acts as the clue to the meaning of Paul, but Paul as the clue to the meaning of Acts.

8

I am not Ashamed of the Gospel

"I am not ashamed of the gospel." Many commentators on Romans have explained these words in a psychological sense. At the beginning of his letter Paul reflects upon the splendour and significance of the place to which his words are addressed, and on its manifest commitment to an understanding of man's existence radically different from his own, and consciously thrusts away the natural feeling of shame which comes upon him at the thought of the figure that he, an obscure provincial bearing a message which must inevitably have appeared unacceptable even if it proved intelligible, must cut in the eyes of the capital. This kind of interpretation has a respectable history. Chrysostom works out at considerable length the contrast between the son of the carpenter and the rulers and gods of Rome. Bengel, more succinctly, writes: "Mundo evangelium est *stultitia* et *infirmitas*. Quare mundi opinione esset erubescendum, Romae praesertim: sed Paulus non erubescit." There is no need to underestimate such psychological factors in the situation, and I should not wish to unsay my own statement of them in my commentary. Paul had probably not read those lines of Vergil's which impressively close J. Weiss's *History of Primitive Christianity*—

> Verum haec tantum alias inter caput extulit urbes
> quantum lenta solent inter viburna cupressi (*Eclogue* 1.24–5)—

but now that ninety years of empire had passed since Vergil wrote them, the sentiment they contained must have become common property. Of this Paul cannot have been unaware.

True, however, as observations of this kind may be, they are not adequate as an explanation of Paul's words. He had not been invited to address the Roman Senate, and neither Vergil's poetry

nor imperial building projects had altered the fact that the back
streets of Rome were pretty much the same as those of other large
towns with which Paul was already familiar—Antioch, Ephesus,
Athens, Corinth; and it was in these that his work, if he reached
Rome, would probably lie. In Rome too it would probably prove
true that the elect did not number many wise (by this world's
standards), many powerful, or many nobly born. No doubt Paul
would feel at home among them. Moreover, the construction of
his sentence is to be observed. He has just stated (1.15) that he
is ready to preach the gospel in Rome, and then adds (1.16) the
ground on which his readiness rests: οὐ γὰρ ἐπαισχύνομαι τὸ
εὐαγγέλιον. That is to say, the not being ashamed of the gospel
is an antecedent condition which is not in itself necessarily connected with the particular circumstances Paul has in mind, though,
when it is applied to them, it constitutes a basis on which his
willingness to undertake Christian activity even at the centre of
the Empire may rest. That Paul was not ashamed of the gospel
was a proposition that had particular relevance and point in a
letter addressed to Rome, but it was not a proposition specially
thought out for the occasion.

This is borne out by the fact that the content of these words
in Romans 1.16 is paralleled elsewhere. Paul does not in any
other passage use the word ἐπαισχύνεσθαι in a similar context
(it occurs only at Romans 6.21, in a quite different setting). The
simple verb αἰσχύνεσθαι, however, occurs at Philippians 1.20,
where I take the context to be a situation in which Paul is awaiting
trial. Whatever happens he will not be put to shame. This is a
safe proposition, for Paul knows that Christ can and will be glorified in his, Paul's, body, εἴτε διὰ ζωῆς, εἴτε διὰ θανάτου. Such
a ground of confidence is in itself a clear indication that not being
ashamed is an antecedent, Christian, rather than a social, condition; its cause lies not in Paul's relation to his environment but in
the nature of the gospel. The same verb (αἰσχύνεσθαι) occurs in
2 Corinthians 10.8, which describes a situation which differs, in
that Paul is here confronted not with pagans but with rivals
inside the Church; the situation is the same, however, in that his
apostleship and his gospel are being put to the test. In these circumstances, Paul affirms confidently, οὐκ αἰσχυνθήσομαι. His
apostleship and his gospel, rooted as they are in God, will stand
the test successfully; his authority, positively exercised, is real,

because it springs not from his own capacity to control his environment but from a divine message and commission.

Paul also uses the verb καταισχύνεσθαι. Romans 5.5; 1 Corinthians 11.4,5,22 are clearly not relevant. 2 Corinthians 7.14; 9.4 are relevant only in that they illustrate the use of the simple verb in 10.8: Paul's boasting about the Corinthian achievement in regard to the collection would reduce him to shame if it were shown to have no substance in it—just as his boasting about his apostolic ἐξουσία would do, if his authority proved to be no more than an empty and baseless claim. In Romans 9.33; 10.11, however, Isaiah 28.16 is quoted, in substantial agreement with the LXX: ὁ πιστεύων ἐπ' αὐτῷ οὐ καταισχυνθήσεται (at 9.33, D G make the agreement complete by substituting οὐ μὴ καταισχυνθῇ). The Hebrew differs, having *lo' yaḥiš* (*shall not make haste*, or, better, *get alarmed*). Again, the sense is that of having a firm standing ground; the metaphor refers now not specifically to the position and authority of a preacher and apostle, but to the standing of any Christian. 1 Corinthians 1.27 puts the same theme as it were in reverse. Judged by normal standards the Christian mob in Corinth might well feel ashamed in the presence of those who, by these standards, were wise, powerful, and nobly born; but these were not God's standards, and in due course it will be the wise, powerful, and noble who are exposed to shame in their frailty and folly. In the same context, 1 Corinthians 2.3 is only an apparent exception to Paul's unashamed confidence in proclaiming the gospel. When he speaks of his weakness, fear, and trembling, this is not because he had in Corinth lost his confidence in the gospel and become ashamed of it, but rather because of his sense of responsibility in proclaiming it (so, for example, Schlatter).

The Deutero-Pauline literature also affords plenty of material of a similar kind which is conveniently disclosed by study of the same words. 1 Peter 4.16 is the classical example of the use of αἰσχύνεσθαι. I must not digress to consider the problem of the persecutions implied by this epistle, and inquire whether ὡς χριστιανός means that persecution "for the name" had already been set upon a legal footing. It is at all events clear that the profession of Christianity was likely to lead to grave consequences (otherwise expressions such as πύρωσις in 4.12, and the "roaring lion" of 5.8, would be ludicrous), and the author urges his readers in these circumstances not to be ashamed of the faith and of the society that had led to their suffering. The use of the cognate noun, αἰσχύνη, in Hebrews 12.2 is equally striking, for the example of Christ himself, who thought nothing of the shame of crucifixion, is invoked to encourage Christians. Paul's ἐπαισχύνεσθαι reappears in important passages in 2 Timothy. Paul himself is represented as not ashamed of his sufferings (1.12); Timothy must not be ashamed either of the testimony of the Lord (that is, he must not through shame draw back from bearing this testimony), or of Paul as a prisoner (1.8); in the latter respect Onesiphorus has set a good example (1.16). 1 Peter 2.6 contains the same quotation from Isaiah 28.16 that appears in Romans 9.33; 10.11; and in 1 Peter 3.16 there is an interesting inversion that reflects though it changes the familiar usage; so far from themselves being ashamed of their Christian profession Christians should so live that their attackers may be put to shame (ἵνα . . . καταισχυνθῶσιν οἱ ἐπηρεάζοντες). Another important inversion occurs at Hebrews 11.16: God is not ashamed of those who trust him.

Hermas (*Similitudes* 8.6.4; 9.21.3) uses ἐπαισχύνεσθαι of the apostates, traitors, and double-minded (ἀποστάται, προδόται, δίψυχοι), who because of their cowardice deny—are ashamed of—the name of their Lord (with a probable allusion to the use of this name in baptism), but outside the Pauline and Deutero-Pauline writings the most important passages are Ignatius, *Smyrnaeans* 10.2 and 1 John 2.28. In the former, Ignatius, noting that the Smyrnaeans have not despised or been ashamed of (ὑπερηφανήσατε, ἐπῃσχύνθητε) his bonds, adds, Neither will our perfect hope, Jesus Christ, be ashamed of you (ὑμᾶς ἐπαισχυνθήσεται). In the latter, John urges his readers to abide in Christ, so that at his manifestation they may have confidence (παρρησία) and not be put to shame (μὴ αἰσχυνθῶμεν) before him (so as to be repulsed from him, ἀπ᾽ αὐτοῦ).

These passages in Ignatius and John are important because they connect a state of things at the present time (which in Ignatius is described as being—or not being—ashamed of the circumstances of Christ's representative) with being put to shame in the presence of Christ, that is (if we may interpret John by Ignatius), through Christ's own being ashamed, at the judgement, of those whose action at an earlier stage had been unworthy of him. These sayings, which are both fairly late in date, thus point with particular clearness to a saying ascribed to Jesus himself in Mark 8.38:

> Whoever is ashamed of me and of my words in this adulterous and sinful generation, of him will the Son of man be ashamed when he comes in the glory of his Father with the holy angels.

In view of the variety of passages we have just considered it should immediately be clear that, whatever the origin and history of this saying may be, it is hardly adequate to say with Loisy, "Paul's mind and even his language reappear".[1] There are Pauline parallels, but the background is wider than Pauline, and in fact this verse sets before us a very complicated and much disputed problem in *Traditionsgeschichte*.

We must begin by noting the synoptic parallels at this point. Matthew 16.27 offers a piece of formalized apocalyptic:

> For the Son of man will come in the glory of his Father with his angels, and then he will repay each man according to his behaviour ($\pi\rho\hat{a}\xi\iota\nu$).

From this saying almost everything distinctive in the Marcan verse has been removed; in particular it lacks the contrast and parallel between being ashamed of Jesus, and the Son of man's being ashamed. That the Matthaean form is secondary is clear; that Matthew was actuated in his editing by the desire to remove the apparent Marcan distinction between Jesus and the Son of man, and to show that Jesus as Son of man was himself the Judge who would hand out rewards and punishments (compare, for example, 25.31) is also clear.

Luke 9.26 does little more than rearrange the Marcan form of the warning:

> Whoever is ashamed of me and of my words, of him will the Son of man be ashamed, when he comes in his glory and that of the Father and of the holy angels.

The adulterous and sinful generation drops out, for Luke is not thinking of one generation only, but of conditions of Christian life that will stretch into the distant future; and the glory is not only the Father's—the Son of man and the angels have their proper glory too. But this is not a point Mark would have wished

---

[1] *Les Évangiles synoptiques* (Ceffonds 1907–8), ii. p. 26.

to contradict: the "great power and glory" of Mark 13.26 are the power and glory of the Son of man.

So far then we find a primary Marcan saying, which Matthew and Luke have modified under no other motivation than their own editorial presuppositions. There is, however, much more to consider. A similar saying occurs in parallel but not identical forms in Matthew and Luke.

Matthew 10.32–3:

> Every one who shall confess me (ὁμολογήσει ἐν ἐμοί) before men, I too will confess him (ὁμολογήσω ἐν αὐτῷ) before my Father who is in heaven. And whoever denies (ἀρνήσηται) me before men, I too will deny (ἀρνήσομαι) before my Father who is in heaven.

Luke 12.8–9:

> I tell you, everyone who confesses me (ὁμολογήσῃ ἐν ἐμοί) before men, the Son of man will confess him (ὁμολογήσει ἐν αὐτῷ) before the angels of God. But he who denies (ὁ ἀρνησάμενος) me before men shall be denied (ἀπαρνηθήσεται) before the angels of God.

Here is a divergent Q form of the Marcan saying. Of this Q form Matthew and Luke give versions that are not identical, but they agree in differing from Mark in the following points:

(*a*) they contain not only a negative warning saying, but also a promise—the confessor will not lose his reward;

(*b*) in the negative saying they speak not of being ashamed but of denying.

They both agree with the Marcan saying, however, in that the language they use is appropriate to the situation of Christians in time of persecution. For confessing (ὁμολογεῖν, ὁμολογία) compare John 9.22; 12.42; Romans 10.9f; 1 Timothy 6.12f; 1 John 2.23; 4.2,3,15; 2 John 7; Hebrews 3.1; 4.14; 10.23 (and cf. Revelation 3.5); and for denying (ἀρνεῖσθαι, ἀπαρνεῖσθαι), in addition to the narratives of Peter's denial, 1 Timothy 5.8; 2 Timothy 2.12; 2 Peter 2.1; 1 John 2.22f; Jude 4; Revelation 2.13; 3.8.

Matthew's is the smoother form of the Q saying, and shows its parallelism most completely:

I

He who confesses me	He who denies me
I will confess	I will deny.

Each clause consists of two precisely parallel members, and the two clauses are parallel with each other. In the Lucan form the parallelism is imperfect in the saying as a whole, and at each stage. The first clause shows the same change from "I" to "Son of man" as the Marcan saying—

He who confesses *me* . . .
The *Son of man* will confess . . .

The parallelism is broken in the second clause also, though not in the same way; an active verb is followed by a passive—

He who denies me . . .
Will be denied . . .

In Matthew, confessing and denying take place before "my Father who is in heaven", in Luke, before "the angels of God".

It is unnecessary to point out that controversy has raged over the relative originality of these sayings, and quite impossible even to outline the course of the discussion; it will, however, be useful to illustrate it. I am not in this paper concerned with literary criticism and form criticism for their own sake, but some attention to them will serve to bring out theological points of value for the comparison of Paul with the synoptic tradition.

The modern phase of the discussion of such questions may be taken to begin with Bultmann's *Geschichte der Synoptischen Tradition*. On p. 117 (cf. p. 134) of the 1931 edition[1] he says that Mark and the original form of the Q saying agree in distinguishing between Jesus and the Son of man; this distinction is primary in comparison with Matthew's direct application of the saying to the person of Jesus; Mark has abbreviated the full (positive and negative) form of the saying under the influence of the context in which he places it; one cannot deduce from Luke 12.9 that the saying originally contained no reference to the Son of man, since Luke elsewhere destroys the parallelism of sayings he transmits. Probably, therefore, though he does not explicitly say so, Bultmann would take the primitive form of the saying to be something like

[1] ET, *The History of the Synoptic Tradition* (1963), p. 112; cf. p. 128.

Whoever confesses me . . .
The Son of man will confess . . .
Whoever denies (or, is ashamed of) me . . .
The Son of man will deny (or, be ashamed of) . . .

When Bultmann returned to the issue in the light of later discussions,[1] he drew attention to the views of C. H. Dodd, E.
Käsemann, and P. Vielhauer. Dodd[2] thinks the Q form, because
of its parallelism, more original, and notes that in it the reference
to the Son of man is less secure; in any case, the Son of man is
not as in Mark described as "coming"—he simply confesses, or
denies, in heaven, "Those who acknowledge Christ on earth
thereby possess the sign that they are eternally accepted by Him"
(p. 94).

Käsemann considers Mark's ἐπαισχύνεσθαι to be a Grecized
version of Q's ὁμολογεῖν ἐν and ἀρνεῖσθαι. Matthew, on the
other hand, is secondary to Mark in that he identifies Jesus and
the Son of man. The Marcan distinction, however (and here
Käsemann appears to go beyond Bultmann), is not sufficient to
show that the saying in this form (or with ἀρνεῖσθαι instead of
ἐπαισχύνεσθαι) goes back to Jesus. It has its place in the sacred
law of the early Church. "This saying has preserved the special
character of Palestinian prophetic discourse, which announces
clauses of sacred law for the community and attaches to earthly
circumstances heavenly blessing or divine curse in the eschatological future."[3]

According to Vielhauer,[4] "it is no longer possible to reconstruct
the original wording of the saying" (p. 69). The Marcan form is
secondary in that it is shortened and contains only the threat and
not the promise, and in its use of ἐπαισχύνεσθαι . It is at least
possible that the passive (ἀπαρνηθήσεται) in Luke's second member is original, and points to God as the subject of the active verb.
If this is so, it means that God will be the agent in the first member
also, and that the reference to Son of man will be a christological
variation—the beginning of a process carried logically through by
Matthew.

---

[1] In the German *Ergänzungsheft* (1959; 1962); E.T., p. 397
[2] *Parables of the Kingdom* (1936), pp. 53f.
[3] *Exegetische Versuche und Besinnungen* (Göttingen 1960, 1964) I, p. 211;
cf. II, p. 102; II, pp. 78f.
[4] *Festschrift für Günther Dehn* (Neukirchen 1957), pp. 68ff.

Bultmann records these suggestions without giving any hint that he is convinced by them. They are well chosen in that they cover between them a good deal of the most important thinking on the subject of recent years. A few additions, however, should be made.

G. Bornkamm[1] thinks it can be asserted with confidence that Jesus spoke (in the manner of Mark 8.38) of the future coming of the Son of man. The distinction between Jesus and the coming Son of man is striking, and gives to Luke 12.8f and Mark 8.38 a strong claim to authority. H. E. Tödt and F. Hahn also follow Bultmann in this respect.

E. Haenchen[2] stands close to Käsemann. He agrees that Mark 8.38 represents a relatively early stage in the use of Son of man, "according to which Jesus is not yet, but only will in the future become, the Son of man" (p. 299). This, however, does not make the saying authentic. Both in Mark and Q it presupposes a situation in which one is asked whether he belongs to the *Jesus-gemeinde*. Some will deny this in order to save their lives. This sort of situation arose in the Church after Easter, but cannot have occurred among the disciples before the crucifixion. "Verse 38 is thus a prophetic admonition belonging within the post-resurrection community" (p. 209).

J. Jeremias[3] brings a different kind of criticism to bear upon the view that Mark 8.38 has as it stands a high claim to authenticity, and thus strikes out on a line different from those we have noted so far. He sets out side by side sayings containing "Son of man" and parallel sayings in which Son of man is replaced by the first person pronoun singular. Discussion shows that the form without Son of man is regularly the older. This observation may be applied to Matthew 10.32f, Luke 12.8f; and the result is that the Matthaean form cannot be dismissed (as many have thought) as secondary to the Lucan.

Some have defended the substantial authenticity of Mark 8.38. V. Taylor thinks it less original than the Q form, and that it may originally have lacked the apocalyptic colouring now visible in verse 38b ("when he comes"). It was nevertheless eschatological.

If the saying is original [and Taylor certainly suggests that he thinks so] one of two possibilities must be true: either, at some

---

[1] *Jesus von Nazareth* (Stuttgart 1957), p. 206.
[2] *Der Weg Jesu* (Berlin 1966), pp. 298ff.   [3] *ZNTW* 58 (1967), p. 170.

point in his ministry, Jesus spoke of the coming of a supernatural Son of Man other than Himself, or by "the Son of
Man" He meant the Elect Community of which He was to be
the Head.[1]

Taylor evidently prefers the latter alternative, and draws the
conclusion that Mark 8.38 is at present out of place.

Dr M. D. Hooker thinks that "we can perhaps trace the development of the saying from Luke 12.8f, through Mark 8.38, to
Matthew 16.27",[2] but thinks that the apparent distinction
between Jesus himself and the Son of man can be defended and
explained without recourse to Taylor's pair of alternatives. In
both verses 34 and 38a (which together form a complete counter-
part to the Q pair) Jesus speaks of himself because "he is speaking
to those who wish to follow him as they know him in his earthly
life" (p. 119). In verse 38b this shifts to the Son of man because
the reference is now to "some future point of time when Jesus
will recognize publicly those who are his followers" (p. 120).
The term Son of man is now used because in the future Jesus'
authority as Son of man will be generally acknowledged. "At
present, his authority is veiled, but when it is revealed, then the
paradox which has brought suffering and shame to both the Son
of man and his disciples will cease, and he will be recognized as
the rightful ruler" (p. 121). It is difficult to see how Jesus could
have proclaimed another as Son of man and have left room for
himself, and "extremely unlikely that the Church would ever have
created a saying in the form found in Mark 8.38" (p. 189).

A somewhat similar view is taken by E. Schweizer in his recent
commentary on Mark.[3] In the Marcan saying, the last clause (in
the glory of his Father with the holy angels) may be discounted
as an explanatory comment from the Church, and Luke 12.8f
may be regarded as the oldest form of the saying. But "The
unusual distinction made between 'I' and 'Son of Man' can be
traced to Jesus, since it was taken for granted by the church that
these were equivalent terms" (p. 100; E.T., p. 178). By the Son
of man, however, Jesus means himself. "This statement is clear

---

[1] *The Gospel according to St Mark* (1952), p. 384.
[2] *The Son of Man in Mark* (1967), p. 119.
[3] *Das Evangelium nach Markus* (NTD 1; Göttingen 1967); E.T., *The Good
News according to Mark* (1970).

if we emphasize that the final judgment will be determined now by the decision of the hearers as they confront the man Jesus. Jesus is speaking of that judgment in modest terms which portray his role objectively" (pp. 100f; E.T., p. 178).

It is now possible finally to make a brief reference to the article on υἱὸς τοῦ ἀνθρώπου by C. Colpe.[1] He thinks (p. 459) that the Marcan saying has been exposed to a good deal of editorial re-writing. His usage shows, however, the Mark had no objection to the words ἀρνεῖσθαι, ἀπαρνεῖσθαι; ἐπαισχύνεσθαι is not Pauline but comes from the common tradition. Mark has added καὶ τοὺς ἐμοὺς λόγους, expanded "before men" into "in this adulterous and sinful generation", and described the coming of the Son of man in traditional apocalyptic terms. In accordance with his general position he has identified the coming Son of man with the earthly Jesus, as his addition of τοῦ πατρὸς αὐτοῦ shows. Colpe agrees with Jeremias in preferring the form without "Son of man" (p. 450).

It will be clear from what has been said that the last word on this question has not yet been spoken—nor will it be spoken in this paper, which after all is primarily about Paul and must soon return to its main theme. When the discussion (of which I have reviewed only a fragment) is surveyed, it appears that some at least have attempted to decide too quickly which is the most primitive form of the saying we are dealing with, and whether this primitive form was spoken by Jesus, or originated in the post-Easter community.

It may be affirmed without hesitation that the saying was current in the Church, probably in several forms, from an early time; the Church, even when not persecuted in a formal sense, was almost always subject to pressures which made it difficult rather than easy to admit one's adherence to the crucified Jesus and his followers, easy rather than difficult to turn one's back on the whole disreputable lot. The use of the odd Greek ὁμολογεῖν ἐν points to a Semitic-speaking background; and it is not impossible[2] that behind the variation of ἀρνεῖσθαι and ἐπαισχύνεσθαι lies the Aramaic pair kᵉp̄ar (to deny, renounce) and hᵃp̄ar (to be ashamed). The absence of the positive member of the Q saying in Mark becomes less striking when, with Miss Hooker, we observe that its substance is contained in 8.34—he who denies

---

[1] *TWNT* 8, pp. 403–81.   [2] See Colpe, *TWNT* 8, p. 450.

himself and takes up his cross is in fact recognized as a disciple. This does not answer the question whether Mark has accommodated the parallel saying to his context, or Q has produced the parallelism out of material in the Marcan form. Fortunately, however, this is precisely the kind of question this paper need not attempt to settle.

The widest divergence of opinion has been expressed over the question whether or not the reference to "Son of man" is original. Two arguments have to be weighed against each other.

(*a*) The primitive Church would not have made up a saying in a form that distinguished between Jesus and the Son of man, whom it identified.

(*b*) "Son of man" is never replaced by "I"; therefore "I" must be original.

Neither of these arguments is or can be entirely satisfactory. On the one hand, we do not know what the primitive Church could or could not do except by observing what it did; and it is a fact that, in its records, when Jesus speaks of the future coming of the Son of man he does so in the third person. On the other hand, it can be alleged that "Son of man" is never replaced by "I" only when all parallels have been discussed and it has been proved in every case that "I" is original and "Son of man" secondary; one must not therefore use the argument, "Son of man" is never replaced by "I", therefore it is not so in this case. The one really firm point is that Matthew, in 16.27, though he does not substitute "I" for "Son of man", does remove the distinction between Jesus and the Son of man; to remove this distinction thus was an editorial tendency, even if not a universal tendency.

There is in fact no form of the saying that has not been edited. "In the glory of his Father with the holy angels" reflects Mark's Son of God Christology. "Before the angels" recalls Luke's interest in angels. "In the presence of my Father who is in heaven" contains a common Matthaean idiom. This editorial process, through which this early saying has passed, is all we need for the moment observe. Some of the theological motifs discernible in the editing will be mentioned later.

One fact stands out clearly: Romans 1.16 stands in close relation with the tradition of the sayings of Jesus, and with a characteristic and early stage of this tradition. When Paul declares that he is not ashamed of the gospel he is not simply putting on a bold front in face of the imperial capital, but expressing solidarity with the early communities which framed their essential discipline in terms of loyalty to Jesus, and saw the Son of man as the one who would execute judgement upon those who by apostasy transgressed this discipline. This fact raises a question which it would be wrong for this gathering to attempt to avoid. If Christianity be defined as the religion that takes its origin in Jesus of Nazareth, what is Paul's place within it? How is he related to Jesus? He has been seen as a second founder, and as a perverter, of the original religion of Jesus. He himself would have regarded neither description as valid. According to him, the Church could rest on one foundation only—Jesus Christ himself; and he had a low opinion of those who built unworthily on that foundation. How does he fare when judged by his own criteria?

This is not a new question, and many of our fathers and grandfathers were convinced that Paul had made of Christianity something that Jesus had never intended. They discussed the question, Jesus or Paul?, and its almost synonymous variant, Jesus or Christ? But the question has often been wrongly put, and when a question is wrongly put a wrong answer is likely and an irrelevant answer certain. Sometimes what may on the surface appear to be the right answer has been given on the wrong grounds. One look into the past may illustrate this point. Wrede writes:

> Julius Wellhausen, the pioneer of Old Testament criticism, has remarked with emphasis that Paul was in truth the man who understood the Gospel of Jesus. Harnack and many others have repeated it. I cannot however assent to this judgement; rather I see in it a considerable historical error.[1]

Wrede seeks to establish his point by first examining supposed connections between the teaching of Jesus and the teaching of Paul. "Without question, it is possible to draw lines of connection from the one to the other; but that does not prove influence on the part of Jesus" (p. 90). That Jesus and Paul were both Jews is sufficient to account for a good deal of similarity. The fact that Paul like Jesus emphasized the supreme command of love is reduced in significance by the consideration that Paul lays less stress on love of the enemy and more on love of the brother, that

[1] W. Wrede, *Paulus* (Tübingen 1907), p. 90.

is, of the fellow-member of the Church; love becomes a *Gemein-detugend* (a social virtue), and this virtue may already have been more emphasized in Diaspora Judaism than we know. It is mistaken to argue that Paul's freedom from the law was due to the example of Jesus. In all his arguments on the subject Paul never appeals to this example; on the contrary, he states that Jesus lived in accordance with the law (Rom. 15.8).

Having destroyed the case for resemblance between the teaching of Jesus and the teaching of Paul, Wrede goes on to demonstrate the differences in a series of contrasting quotations, which, he says, are central on either side. I give only the first pair (p. 93).

Jesus says, You shall be perfect, as your heavenly Father is perfect.

Paul says, He who spared not his own Son, how should he not also with him freely give us all things?

The fact is that the message of Jesus takes the characteristic form of an imperative addressed to the individual. Paul, on the other hand, speaks of a divine act, or rather of a series of divine actions, on the basis of which salvation, as a goal already achieved, is offered to all men.

Of that which, for Paul, is all and everything, Jesus knows— nothing at all. Paul on the other hand certainly shows a series of points of contact with sayings of Jesus; but for Paul all of these belong to things of the second rank, and the kernel of his Gospel lies elsewhere (p. 94).

Wrede is here making a comparison between the recorded and reconstructed teaching of Jesus, and the writing of Paul. Those of his generation who reached conclusions opposite to his did the same thing. Both were wrong, for this was not the kind of connection with Jesus that Paul would have been anxious to claim. H. J. Schoeps quotes aptly from Kümmel:

Paul does not feel himself to be a disciple of the historical Jesus, but a man commissioned by the risen Lord. Hence it is not his mission to hand on the traditions he has received about the historical Jesus and his teaching, but to proclaim the Christ.[1]

This is undoubtedly true. Schoeps has himself, in a chapter

[1] H. J. Schoeps, *Paulus* (Tübingen 1959), p. 51; E.T., *Paul* (1961), p. 57.

heading, rightly described Paul as a "thinker of the post-messianic situation". It is not necessary here to discuss how far the crucifixion and resurrection may have been foreseen and foretold in the teaching of Jesus, and in what ways, if foreseen, they may have been interpreted. Certainly they were, from that point of view, future events, and equally certainly for Paul they were events of the past, and they were eschatologically interpreted. An hour had struck on the clock of history, battle had been joined and a victory won, and things could never be the same again. Paul lived in a new—a post-messianic—situation. It was unthinkable that he should simply transmit the teaching of Jesus. That this teaching was given in a Palestinian setting, whereas Paul lived and preached in the Hellenistic world, is significant enough, but it is far less important than the fact that Paul lived and preached in an eschatologically different world. All the promises of God had been fulfilled in Jesus: old things had passed away, new things had come into being.

I have argued this point elsewhere, especially in relation to the different viewpoint adopted by B. Gerhardsson,[1] and I do not intend to elaborate the theme again. Nor do I mean to retract what I have said if I now add that it seems to me that there is a further point to consider. The question we have to ask about Paul is not whether, in relation to Jesus, he played the role of the plastered cistern, losing not a drop of his master's teaching but faithfully handing it on, and, if interpreting it, interpreting it only in accordance with the decisions of the authorized Christian Sanhedrin in Jerusalem. We have rather to ask whether in his theology he affords a valid interpretation of the total event of Jesus Christ. We must not expect Paul to use the terminology that Jesus used, or be surprised when he drops the vivid pictorial language of the Palestinian parables, and speaks never of the Son of man and seldom of the kingdom, but instead of justification, the Spirit, and the Church. Again, if we are to speak of the "total event of Jesus Christ", we must not be surprised if Paul lays heavy weight on the crucifixion and resurrection. To one who looked back at the story of Jesus through the Easter events and the passion, these must inevitably have appeared not only the nearest but also the most significant elements in the total event. Moreover, if the Easter faith was true, nothing could conceivably be of greater

---

[1] Especially *Memory and Manuscript* (Acta Seminarii Neotestamentici Upsaliensis XXII; Uppsala 1961).

importance, not simply because it meant a staggering and un-precedented act of divine power, but because it meant the dawn of the age to come. Representatively, the messianic affliction was ended in the cross; representatively, the new age had begun with the resurrection. But—and this is the new point I now want to make—though crucifixion and resurrection were evidently the outstanding elements in the total event, they were not the only elements. Jesus was a teacher, and even if his teaching activity is thought of as in part a façade behind which something more profound was concealed, it is hard to think of a faithful and satis-factory interpretation of the whole that failed to do justice to this part of it. Hence the special importance of the contact between Paul and that piece of the gospel traditional material that we are here investigating.

Paul says, "I am not ashamed of the gospel", and though he attaches to the word gospel a meaning that is very different from "an account of the life and teaching of Jesus", there are a few passages where it seems that he is aware of a relation between the two. Foremost, perhaps, of these is Galatians 2.2. Why did Paul submit his gospel to the Jerusalem authorities? With this question we may put another: Why did he take the trouble to visit (ἱστορῆσαι) Cephas (Gal. 1.18)? It is surely evident that he did not regard Cephas and his colleagues as ecclesiastical authorities who had a right to exact obedience in virtue of their office (2.6,11). It is part of an answer to this question that they were the leaders of the Jewish branch of the Church with which he was anxious to keep the peace; if we ask for any further qualification on their part, it can only be that they knew what Jesus had taught. Presumably we may add to this observation that, since these witnesses added nothing (2.6) to Paul, they at least did not consider that his preaching was inconsistent with what they had heard Jesus say.

Other passages indicate that what Paul understood by "the gospel" was capable of being formulated in terms that could be believed, obeyed, accepted, or rejected. 1 Corinthians 9.14 is interesting, though it actually says less than it hints at. The Lord himself gave charge for those who preach the gospel, that they should live by the gospel. This is presumably a reference to

Matthew 10.10: ἄξιος ὁ ἐργάτης τῆς τροφῆς αὐτοῦ
Luke 10.7: ἄξιος ὁ ἐργάτης τοῦ μισθοῦ αὐτοῦ

—a saying in the Q account of the mission of the disciples. Paul does not here describe the teaching of Jesus as εὐαγγέλιον, but he shows that he participates in the process (which can be seen clearly in Mark, and was pointed out by Wellhausen[1]) by which the word εὐαγγέλιον was read back into the narratives as a description of the preaching of Jesus. This means that Paul saw—or believed that he could see—a relation between the content of his preaching and the content of the preaching and teaching of Jesus.

It is not possible, nor would it necessarily be profitable, to examine this conviction of Paul's in general terms. Our attention is directed to a particular passage of his (Rom. 1.16), and this in turn has led us to a parallel group of passages in the teaching of Jesus—more accurately, to one sector of the tradition of the teaching of Jesus. It will take us all the time at our disposal to examine this contact and assess its importance, and this examination will suggest representative material that may lead to general conclusions. The next step is to return to Mark 8.38 and the parallels, and make use of our earlier studies, and other methods, to assess the theological content of the tradition.

The Marcan saying opens: ὃς γὰρ ἐὰν ἐπαισχυνθῇ με καὶ τοὺς ἐμοὺς λόγους. The Q saying has no reference to words; it is only the person of Jesus that is confessed or denied. In Mark the noun λόγους is omitted (according to Nestle's apparatus) by W k* cop Tert. In the Lucan parallel there is similar evidence for omission in D a e l syᶜ Or; but since Luke is certainly secondary to Mark, we need not pursue this variant. The effect of the omission is that the masculine adjective ἐμούς is left without a noun, and must therefore refer to persons: "Whoever is ashamed of me and mine . . .". In both Gospels this reading has been taken seriously and indeed preferred by the *New English Bible*, and it may therefore be reasonable to consider it for a moment. In fact, it will not stand up to examination. It is best to begin with the patristic evidence. Tertullian appears to refer to Mark 8.38 in three places, and to Luke 9.26 in one (it is not clear why the apparatus does not refer to Tertullian at Luke 9.26 as well as at Mark 8.38). It is clear what is happening at *De Fuga* 7. The main point is drawn from the positive element in the Q saying:

[1] J. Wellhausen, *Einleitung in die drei ersten Evangelien* (Berlin 1905), pp. 110ff.

Qui confessus fuerit me, et ego confitebor illum coram patre meo. Quomodo confitebitur fugiens, quomodo fugiet confitens?

Having made this point, Tertullian goes on to quote the negative member, evidently from memory and under the influence of the passage just cited:

Qui mei confusus fuerit, et ego confundar eius coram patre.

This is not to be taken as a serious witness to a variant, and in any case it does not support the reading καὶ τοὺς ἐμούς. In *De Carne Christi* 5 the argument turns upon the reality of Christ's human nature, and it is not surprising that again interest focuses upon the person of Christ to the exclusion of καὶ τοὺς ἐμοὺς λόγους (the whole phrase):

Qui me, inquit, confusus fuerit, confundar et ego eius.

In *De Idololatria* 13 the point is that to commit idolatry is to be ashamed of God. You may be known to be a Christian or not; it makes no difference.

Certe sive hac, sive illac, reus est confusionis in Deo. Qui autem confusus super me fuerit penes homines, et ego confundar super illo, inquit, penes patrem meum, qui est in coelis.

Here Tertullian has confused Mark with Matthew. In *Adversus Marcionem* 4. 21 Tertullian must be quoting not Mark but Luke, since his argument is intended to confound Marcion with Marcion's own gospel. The theme is the shame Christ endured through accepting the conditions of ordinary human birth, life, and death.

Qui confusus, inquit, me fuerit, et ego confundar eius. Quando nec confusionis materia conveniat, nisi meo Christo: cuius ordo magis pudendus, ut etiam haereticorum conviciis pateat, omnem nativitatis et educationis foeditatem, et ipsius etiam carnis indignitatem, quanta amaritudine possunt, perorantibus.

There is no room here for a reference either to *my words* or to *my people*, and they do not appear.

It is worth noting that at Mark 8.38 the extraordinary Old Latin Ms. k actually reads:

Qui autem me confessus fuerit et meos in natione adultera et peccatrice et filios [*sic*] hominis confundetur illum cum venerit in claritate patris sui cum angelis sanctis.

A corrector has erased *et meos*; and of course *confessus* is an error for *confusus* (arising under the influence of Matthew 10.32; Luke 12.8).[1]

Study of these texts not only suffices to make it impossible to take "me and mine" as the original text; it also throws light on the way in which the saying has developed. In the first place, it is evident that conflation and assimilation have been at work. Passages such as Mark 8.38; Matthew 10.32f; Luke 12.8f invite confusion, and are in patristic quotations often confused. In the second place, there was a natural concentration of interest upon the person of Christ, not only because this was for Christians the centre of loyalty, but also because it was the point of attack for non-Christians, who naturally found the crucified sophist not merely unimpressive but offensive to their natural theological presuppositions. For the same reason this was also the point of dangerous modification for unorthodox Christians who wished to accommodate Christian belief to current objections by denying the full offensive reality of the human person Jesus of Nazareth.

With these considerations in mind we can accept without hesitation as the earliest form preserved in the extant Gospels the Marcan με καὶ τοὺς ἐμοὺς λόγους. Compare Mark 10.29: ἕνεκεν ἐμοῦ καὶ ἕνεκεν τοῦ εὐαγγελίου. Romans 1.16, however, was written before Mark, and we may ask whether Paul does not suggest an earlier stage of the tradition which referred only to "words" or "gospel", and contained no "me". This is not impossible, and it is worth noting that it would not have the effect of reducing the christological significance of the saying. Paul was certainly not a less christological thinker than Mark. To suffer on behalf of Jesus might indicate no more than the measure of personal affection and loyalty that any one of us might feel for another; but to suffer on behalf of the words of Jesus, or of the gospel (whether one thinks of this as the gospel he preached, or as the gospel which has him at its centre) means recognizing that he was the bearer of the word of God, and thus the unique agent of God—a more profound belief than the conviction that he was a lovable person possessed of the powers of leadership. Thus, "I am

[1] On this reading see J. Wordsworth, W. Sanday, and H. J. White, *Old Latin Biblical Texts* II (1886), p. xci.

not ashamed of the gospel" carries with it, "I am not ashamed of Christ and the gospel". This is not to say that "I am not ashamed of the gospel" was not an earlier formulation than "I am not ashamed of Christ and the gospel"; Romans 1.16 may suggest that it was, though this earlier formulation has left no trace in the Gospels. This reflection must add weight to the argument that in the second, retributive, clause, "Son of man" is original. To this clause we now turn.

I shall not pursue further the question whether or not this clause originally contained a reference to the Son of man, but inquire what sort of event is implied by the denying, or being ashamed, referred to. Future verbs—ἐπαισχυνθήσεται, ἀποδώσει (cf. μέλλει ἔρχεσθαι), ἀρνήσομαι, ἀπαρνηθήσεται—are used throughout, but those in the Q saying are capable of a different interpretation from those in the Marcan. Q can be taken as a simple logical future: If A does X, B will do Y. B's action is future in that it is contingent upon what A does, but it is thought of as essentially a continuation of A's action in the present. Deny Christ, and you will be denied—as in 2 Timothy 2.12 (εἰ ἀρνησό-μεθα, κἀκεῖνος ἀρνήσεται ἡμᾶς). Mark (followed by Matthew and Luke) clearly goes beyond this, and describes an event that will take place at a specific time in the future. Retribution is indeed directly and necessarily connected with the offence, but does not follow immediately in point of time. The offence takes place in this generation, and the retribution at a time specified by a temporal clause, ὅταν ἔλθῃ—certainly not now.

Of all the five passages concerned, Matthew 16.27 gives the clearest picture of a judgement scene: the Son of man will come in glory and recompense each man according to his behaviour. The scene is familiar and indeed formalized (cf. Matt. 25.31). Matthew has clarified but not misunderstood what Mark intended to convey; Mark too, followed closely by Luke, thinks of a judgement scene. The only difference is that in Matthew the Son of man is the judge, whereas in Mark and Luke it is not clear whether he is judge, witness, or counsel for the prosecution. ἐπαισχύνεσθαι is perhaps a word that suits a witness better than a judge. There is a somewhat similar problem in 1 Enoch, especially in chapters 62 and 63, where the kings and the mighty appear for judgement. "They shall be downcast of countenance" (62.5), "their faces shall be filled with shame" (10), "their faces shall be filled with darkness and shame before that Son of man" (63.11). But it is not clear precisely what role that Son of man plays. At the beginning of chapter 62 the Lord of Spirits seats him on the throne of his glory and the spirit of righteousness is poured out upon him (62.2); apparently he is to act as judge. This view of the Son of man lasts up to 62.9, where the kings and the mighty petition him and supplicate for mercy at his hands. But the next verse continues: "Nevertheless that Lord of Spirits will so press them that they shall hastily go forth from his presence, and their faces shall be filled with shame, and darkness shall grow deeper on their faces." In 63.1 it is the Lord of spirits whom the mighty and the kings implore to grant them a little respite, but in verse 11 follow the words quoted above, in which once more the Son of man appears to be acting as judge. It is not unreasonable to infer a measure of uncertainty about the role of the Son of man in the judgement.

Matthew in general has a much more clear-cut picture of the Son of man than Mark. For Matthew the Son of man is a king and has a kingdom, and he acts as judge (13.41; 16.28; 19.28; 25.31). There is in Mark no passage that so unambiguously states the judgeship and kingship of the Son of man. 14.62, where the Son of man sits on the right hand of the Power and comes with the clouds of heaven, perhaps implies so much, but does not explicitly claim it. We are in fact dealing here with a theme discussed—though without reference to our material—by C. F. D. Moule[1] in "From Defendant to Judge—and Deliverer: an Enquiry into the use and limitations of the theme of vindication in the New Testament". It is in Matthew, not in Mark, that the Son of man becomes in a full sense the Judge and Deliverer. It would, however, be wrong to suppose that this transition is simply a function of developing Christology, which progressively exalts the figure of Jesus. All the Gospels insist upon a Defendant figure, and do so because they identify the Son of man with Jesus, a human figure who really did stand trial before his fellow-countrymen, not only when he appeared before the Sanhedrin but throughout his ministry as he exposed himself and his teaching—his words— to the approbation or scorn of any who chose to listen and to observe. In 8.38, Mark—and that in this he is more primitive than Matthew is scarcely open to doubt—allows this description of the Son of man to persist in the account of the heavenly trial

---

[1] In *S.N.T.S. Bulletin* III (1952), pp. 40–53.

scene. Even now, if ἐπαισχύνεσθαι is to be taken seriously, the scene is not an entirely victorious one for the Son of man, for he is ashamed, ashamed to recognize those who profess to be his disciples. That is, he is called upon as witness to answer the question: Are these men, who profess to be so, truly yours? And must answer in confusion: No, indeed; I am ashamed that they should take my name on their lips.

To go so far, however, is to vindicate Mark's allusive picture of a court and judgement scene, and thus also his ὅταν. The ἔλθῃ that accompanies ὅταν is presumably based upon Daniel 7.13. The same passage may not unreasonably be taken to supply δόξα (Dan. 7.14,LXX: πᾶσα δόξα αὐτῷ λατρεύουσα), and perhaps the angels (7.13,LXX: οἱ παρεστηκότες παρῆσαν αὐτῷ). There remains for consideration only the reference to "his Father". The Son of man is represented as Son of God. In this Mark is followed by Luke. The important point to observe is that Mark 8.38 stands in the course of a long and carefully worked out paragraph in which Marks sets forth the relation between the three concepts: Messiah, Son of man, and Son of God. All are fulfilled in Jesus. Peter confesses him to be the Christ; this identification is not rejected but for the moment set aside; it is hinted at again in the Transfiguration narrative. Instead Jesus affirms that he is the Son of man, and will, in that role, suffer rejection and contumely, though his suffering and death will be followed by resurrection. At the time of vindication, however, it will be impossible for disciples to join him; if they do not share his reproach now, they will have no share in his glory hereafter, when he is manifested not only as the glorious Son of man but as the Son of God, in the glory of his Father. This will happen soon: some of those present, notwithstanding the impending suffering, will live to see it. At this point Mark attaches the Transfiguration, going out of his way to relate it to what precedes by a reference, unique in the main part of his Gospel, to a precise interval: after six days. This narrative has been rightly explained by G. H. Boobyer[1] as an anticipation of the parousia, in which the Son of man appears with the clouds, accompanied by the holy ones. In the course of it Jesus is addressed as the Son of God, whose word must be heard and obeyed. All this, however, must for the moment, until the resurrection, be kept secret. Jesus is not to be followed because of

[1] *St Mark and the Transfiguration Story* (1942).

the glory to which he will eventually lead his followers, but simply for his own sake, and the gospel's.

This is essentially a Marcan construction: 8.27—9.9(13) sets out Mark's own gospel more plainly than any other part of his book. How far certain parts of it correspond with historical fact is a question of notorious difficulty. Was the title Christ used of Jesus? by Jesus? was it accepted by him? Did he use the term Son of man to describe himself in his earthly life, or did he (if he used it at all) use it only of someone else? Did he foresee and interpret his impending death? What sort of role did he predict for his followers? What sort of vision was the Transfiguration? Questions such as these can only be answered, if they can be answered at all, when the passage before us is set in the context of the Gospel material as a whole, and at this stage in our study (which, I must repeat, is not primarily aimed at the interpretation of the Gospels for their own sake) there is only one aspect of this comparison that can be mentioned. This, however, is the most important. The theme of the whole paragraph is focused in Mark 8.38, and in the affirmation that there exists a unique, mysterious, but organic relation between the obscurity and humiliation of the ministry of Jesus, and the glorious future; a relation that may be indifferently described in terms of the coming of the Son of man (with features based on Daniel 7 and echoing parts of 1 Enoch) and of the establishing of the kingdom of God in power. Mark as a whole uses both methods of expressing the relation between a present, which is unique because it is bound up with a particular historical figure, and a future, which also is unique because it is the end of history. On the one hand, Jesus is the Son of man, and the compound Jesus–Son of man figure has a continuous history which begins with an earthly ministry, continues through rejection, suffering, and death to resurrection, and ultimately to parousia and judgement, when the elect are gathered together from the ends of the earth to rejoice with the Son of man. On the other hand, the kingdom of God, whose future coming in power is accepted in the ordinary Jewish apocalyptic manner, receives a preliminary manifestation during the ministry of Jesus as he casts out demons and thus overthrows the strong man who hitherto has enjoyed undisputed control of what he has been pleased to regard as his property. The organic relation between the mysterious present and the glorious future manifestation of the kingdom is expressed notably in the parables about seeds and their growth. The ministry of Jesus may be as small and insignificant as a mustard seed, yet it is as closely related to the future consummation as the mustard seed is to the large mustard plant.

It has been pointed out in a familiar and important study, and subsequently often repeated, that these two strands of tradition, the one relating to the Son of man and the other to the kingdom of God, are distinct from each other, and from this observation historical inferences, which may or may not be justifiable, have been drawn. With such inferences we are not at present concerned. What matters is that the two great strata of the Gospel tradition—the Son of man stratum and the kingdom of God stratum—are agreed in their fundamental representation of the significance of the historic ministry of Jesus. This observation may lead us back directly to Paul.

What is the theological significance of this traditional interpretation of the ministry? It is not worked out in theological terms in the Synoptic Gospels, and we shall therefore have to work it out for ourselves. When we have done so, we shall be able to see whether the external and formal relation to the tradition of Paul's οὐ γὰρ ἐπαισχύνομαι is backed by a valid understanding of its theological substance.

The following points can be made. It will hardly be necessary to bring out step by step their relevance to Romans 1.16.

1. The traditional material sees a unique power, a δύναμις, at work in the ministry. This is manifested in miracles, which are characteristically described as δυνάμεις, and are regarded as signs of the kingdom of God (Matt. 12.28; Luke 11.20). This δύναμις is at times crudely described as a kind of quasi-physical fluid operating through contact with Jesus or even with his clothing (e.g. Mark 5.27), having clear connection with magic (Mark 7.33; 8.23). It is also expressed in other manifestations of the ἐξουσία of Jesus, such as his teaching (Mark 1.22,27), and his power to command men and secure their obedience (1.17; 2.14). This δύναμις and ἐξουσία come from God (11.27–33, in the whole context). To some extent at least they are transferable, and the disciples are sent out suitably equipped (6.7). The word δύναμις is also used in strictly futuristic eschatological contexts. The clearest examples are Mark 9.1, where it is said that the kingdom

will come ἐν δυνάμει, and 13.26, where the Son of man comes μετὰ δυνάμεως πολλῆς καὶ δόξης (cf. 8.38). The power is the same, but whereas in the present it is secret, in the future it will be manifest. This future manifestation may be described as salvation. It is true that the word σωτηρία does not occur in Matthew and Mark, and that the occurrences in Luke are not clear references to the future (though 1.69,71,77 are eschatological in their formulation); it is true also that the verb σώζειν is used in a variety of senses, some of which amount to little more than "cure". But Mark 8.35; 10.26; 13.13,20 have a clear reference to salvation at the last day. The man who endures to the end will come safely through the convulsive struggles of the dying age, and receive eternal life in the age to come. That is, the primary theme of the Gospel tradition can be described as δύναμις εἰς σωτηρίαν—a power, at present only dimly revealed, which points towards and leads to God's final act of salvation. This δύναμις is what Jesus proclaims—his εὐαγγέλιον, if we may accept the word of Mark 1.14f, etc.

2. I have already said that this δύναμις is only obscurely manifested. This is perhaps an understatement. According to Mark, it was often deliberately concealed by Jesus, and when he was asked to account for his ἐξουσία he refused to do more than hint, by way of an allusion to John the Baptist, at its divine origin. More than this, the words in which he proclaimed his εὐαγγέλιον were, by the best authorities, judged blasphemous and condemned; on the ground of them he was himself condemned to death, and, when executed, proved unable or unwilling to apply the divine σωτηρία to his own case: ἄλλους ἔσωσεν, ἑαυτὸν οὐ δύναται σῶσαι (15.31). The miracles themselves could easily be discounted, and more than discounted; the man was in league with the devil and practised black magic.

From such a person—a cheap wizard, a strolling exorcist, who when put to the test could not use the powers he was supposed to claim—it was natural to turn away in disgust, and to disavow any connection with him one might ever have had. If a different, positive, attitude were taken it could not be on the basis of observed and convincing phenomena. Even the miracles, as we have seen, could prove nothing, and it is evident that most of the inhabitants of Palestine were not impressed by them. There were indeed some who pierced the anonymity of Jesus, or rather had the secret revealed to them, and not by flesh and blood. These were on the whole the babes, and the outcasts of Israel, not those who could parade learning or good works. Even these, it is true, found in the end that the strain was too great, and when the matter came to arrest, trial, and execution, ran away and even denied the Master. The opposite, however, to this negative reaction meant a willingness to trust in a divine secret (Mark 4.11; cf. Matt. 11.25 = Luke 10.21; Matt. 16.17), to deny not the Master but oneself, to follow him at any cost, in obedience and confident trust (Mark 8.34). The single word that expresses this attitude is πίστις. The earlier synoptic passages use this word in the sense of a confidence that Jesus is able to deal with all circumstances, such as illness, storms, and the like. But the verb is used in a way that reflects the theological usage in Paul. Thus in his opening proclamation Jesus summons his hearers: πιστεύετε ἐν τῷ εὐαγγελίῳ. This is the precise opposite of being ashamed of him and his words. At 15.32 πιστεύειν denotes a false faith which requires a demonstration of power in a form which destroys the very nature of the δύναμις in question: καταβάτω νῦν ἀπὸ τοῦ σταυροῦ, ἵνα ἴδωμεν καὶ πιστεύσωμεν. Compare the refusal of a sign in Mark 8.11ff. Thus, if the story of Jesus means the power of God moving towards (εἰς) salvation, it has this meaning to faith—παντὶ τῷ πιστεύοντι.

3. The end point of the process which our material describes is judgement. Matthew 16.27 expresses this precisely, but, as we have seen, Mark 8.38 conveys the same notion clearly enough. Whether the Son of man is judge, or the Father, with the Son of man as witness or advocate, the result is the same: judgement there will be, and the result of the judgement will be determined not by the attitude of the persons in question then (when they may cry Lord, Lord, in vain—Matt. 7.21), but by their earlier attitude to the obscure and humiliated Jesus, that is by their shame or denying, their confessing or faith. That is, there will be a future judgement, but its verdict is already anticipated in the present, and is determined positively or negatively by faith or by the opposite of faith, that is, by a positive or negative relation with Jesus. This appears to correspond with what Paul means by the manifestation of God's righteousness which is the ground of the

Gospel (Romans 1.17; the gospel is God's power leading to salvation, δικαιοσύνη γὰρ θεοῦ ἐν αὐτῷ ἀποκαλύπτεται), and by justification by faith. No more in Paul than in the teaching of Jesus can this lead to moral indifferentism, since faith means obedience (compare, for example, the ὑπακοὴ πίστεως of Romans 1.5), or following Christ with complete denial of self (Mark 8.34). The contrast cited above from Wrede breaks down at this point. The imperative of Jesus rests upon an implicit and occasionally explicit indicative of divine grace, and the Pauline indicative issues in an imperative.

4. There is one word more to say here, but it is not easy to express it except in negative terms. The Marcan paragraph identifies Jesus, the Son of man, and the Son of God, even though in Mark 8.38 the reference to "his Father" is probably editorial, and the verse as it stands appears to bear witness to an earlier stage in the tradition in which Jesus and the Son of man were distinguished. Even, however, when we go back to the earliest stage we can reach and the christological titles become problematical, the figure of Jesus remains central, because it is by men's attitude to, and relation with, him that they are judged; and this is more significant than most formal christological statements. It is reflected in Romans 1.16f, through the doctrine of justification, which is a christological doctrine, but for a clearer parallel we may turn back to Romans 1.3f, which reveals precisely the same uneven continuity between him who lives a human life as the Son of David and him who after his resurrection is exalted to be the Son of God. The same person is both, and it is on the basis of historical confrontation with Jesus (in his word) that final judgement takes place. Here are the essentials of New Testament Christology. They are not in the first instance metaphysical, but show the two ways in which God confronts men; and in them Paul and the gospel tradition are agreed.

This proposition must not be exaggerated. The relation between Paul and the gospel tradition is very complicated, and raises many questions that have not been touched on in this paper. But the present investigation has added some support to the similar conclusions of Jeremias:

It was Paul's greatness that he understood the message of

Jesus as no other New Testament writer did. He was the faithful interpreter of Jesus. This is especially true of his doctrine of justification. It is not of his own making but in its substance conveys the central message of Jesus, as it is condensed in the first beatitude: "Blessed are you poor, for yours is the kingdom of God"[1]

and of E. Käsemann:

It is this [the righteousness of God] for which those referred to by the fourth beatitude have been hungering and thirsting—for the realization of the divine justice on and to our earth. But exactly the same thing seems to me to be happening in the Pauline doctrine of God's righteousness and our justification.[2]

The support is given by the measure of literary and historical contact we have observed between the gospel tradition and words which are often rightly taken to be the kernel of Paul's gospel, which δύναμις θεοῦ ἐστιν πᾶσιν τοῖς πιστεύουσιν.

[1] *The Central Message of the New Testament* (1965), p. 70.
[2] *Versuche* II (see note 3 on p. 123), pp. 102f; E.T. *New Testament Questions of Today* (1969), p. 105.

9

Theology in the World of Learning[1]

If this title appears to suggest a claim on my part to be familiar
with the whole world of learning, I apologize for it; I make no
such claim. I have, however, studied a few things in addition to
theology, and I practise my theology in the setting of a university
which casts its net fairly widely over the whole realm of human
thought and activity; and this means that I am aware, as we all
are, of the pressures that affect all who learn and all who teach
theology in these days—pressures from without that act along
with tensions that arise within, and lead us, often enough, to
question the validity and the value of what we do. I have not the
least thought that in a short address today I shall be able to ease
all these pressures and tensions; nor indeed should I particularly
wish to do so. A certain amount of tension is a healthy thing to
live with, and I should not like to encourage the students of
theology—or the teachers of theology—in this Hall to settle down
to too comfortable an existence. But I should like to look at some
of the problems that arise, and to do something, if I can, to justify
theology as an academic discipline.

That last sentence may call for qualification. I should be the
last man to suggest that the work of a theological hall, that theology
itself, is simply a matter of academic discipline. We are concerned
with far more than that; but it will, I hope, appear that the "far
more" is best achieved not by ignoring academic discipline, but
by treating the academic discipline with the seriousness that it
deserves.

Universities in general are in these days going through a period
of turbulence and unrest; those of us who live in them are not
always very clear what the turbulence and unrest are about, and
we all tend to become sensitive to the charge that we are reac-

[1] An address delivered at the Inaugural Service of the Theological Hall,
Queen's College, Melbourne, on 29 April 1969.

tionary conservatives, and sometimes to join in the quest of change for change's sake. For my part, I believe that the best of the unrest, and its more sober manifestations, are not unrelated to the essence of what universities have always been—or rather, of what universities ought always to have been, of what in their best periods they have approximated to: I mean, the corporate pursuit of truth by communities of committed persons. The old European universities differed in their origins: some were universities of masters, others of scholars, but in each case the one class implied the existence of the other, and the overall effect was the same. A group of persons was engaged in a common quest; some were older, some younger, some experienced, some inexperienced. The younger learned facts and method from the older, the older gained zest and inspiration, and new ideas, from the younger; but for all the goal was the same—"still climbing after knowledge infinite".

Universities and other places of learning have often fallen below their own ideals, but in their best moments they have cherished the aim—inherited from the ancient Greek world, budding in the medieval awakening, bursting into full flower in the Renaissance and again in the Enlightenment—of following the question wherever it might lead, and pursuing knowledge and understanding in complete freedom from prejudice. Anything that threatens these objectives, whether it be a political situation pressing from above or from below, or our own indolence and cowardice, threatens the very existence of universities and of learning itself.

It is the essence of higher education that it introduces students to a world of intellectual responsibility and intellectual discovery in which they are to play their part. . . . The element of partnership between teacher and taught in a common pursuit of knowledge and understanding, present to some extent in all education, should become the dominant element as the student matures and as the intellectual level of work done rises. In the graduate school there are no ultimate authorities, no orthodoxies to which the pupil must subscribe, and he finds himself taking his part, however humbly and modestly, in the task of making experience intelligible and illuminating areas of ignorance. . . . The student needs from the beginning to be made aware of the scope of his subject and to realize that he is not being presented

L

with a mass of information but initiated into a realm of free inquiry.[1]

Now it is these old and lasting truths about university life and the world of learning that put a question mark beside the study of theology. Newer kinds of pressure need not trouble us. Of course, the science and technology faculties will grow larger in proportion to ours; we have nothing to complain of here. And we have no need to fear the new questions that are being asked about the relation and the responsibility of the world of learning to surrounding society. If we have not had at least as much practice as our colleagues in other subjects in relating ourselves and our studies to the world outside the ivory tower, it is our own fault; there are plenty of opportunities. Indeed, we may proceed immediately from this to the first of the two great objections that may be made against theology as an academic discipline. It may be, and has been, argued, that academic study means the pursuit of truth for its own sake, and is therefore not vocational training; whereas theology as we practise it, especially in theological halls and colleges, is nothing if it is not vocational training for the minister. I shall say more about this in a moment; for the present let me go on to state the second great objection to theology as an academic subject. Academic learning, as we have seen, means the free and unprejudiced pursuit of truth. But the theologian (so the argument will run) can make no claim to be unprejudiced. If he were to claim freedom from prejudice, he would thereby proclaim his own apostasy from the Christian faith, which professes to be or to contain or to be founded on a plenary revelation from the fountain of all truth. Surely a Christian theology must begin with a dogmatic assertion, a prior faith, independent of logical analysis; it thus contains at its heart a denial of academic freedom. The alternative is for theology to deny its own origin, to cut its own throat. As Kierkegaard put it, "to be a professor of theology, is to have crucified Christ".

These two allegations, of vocational preoccupation and dogmatic prejudice, are supported by a quantity of prima facie evidence. The young minister, when he leaves college, proceeds to preach week by week the theology he has learnt: to use the arguments he has heard from our philosophers, to teach the biblical history

[1] Higher Education—*Report of the Committee under the Chairmanship of Lord Robbins* (1963), §§ 555f.

and interpretation he has acquired in our biblical classes. The more practical aspects of vocational training—the art, for example, of holding a baby the right way up for baptism, and of conducting a funeral without falling into the grave—we need not concern ourselves with. It is the fact that a man will expect to get much of his stock-in-trade as a preacher of the Word of God from his theological course; and those who teach him would be disappointed if it were otherwise. So also with the second and more serious charge that theology is in its very nature a contradiction of the principle of academic freedom. The historian will have no difficulty in putting his finger on many a theologian whose behaviour has been, in the worst sense of the word, dogmatic, who has been ready to stifle new truth rather than run the risk of allowing it to upset cherished formulas. If I may do so without impiety, I will cite the words of William van Mildert, founder of my own University, Bishop of Durham, and formerly Professor at Oxford, who commended his own church on the ground that it provided "Creeds, Confessions, Catechisms, Formularies of every description . . .: nothing essential is unprovided for, nothing is left to the arbitrary constructions or wandering imaginations of individual instructors".[1] Here was a man, honest, sincere, intelligent, beneficent, and quite incorruptible, who in his own person exemplifies the potential reality of the charges brought against theology as an academic subject.

I hope I have made clear, not least for the benefit of young theologians, who should ponder these things, that there is a prima facie case for banishing theology from the world of humane studies, and relegating it to the realm of prejudice and propaganda. But to go even so far as this is to utter a colossal paradox, for historically theology was in at the foundation of humane studies in the modern sense. The earliest Italian universities, such as Salerno and Bologna, were the creation of the doctors and the lawyers, and, in addition to Arts, their first faculties were of medicine and law; but further north the universities sprang for the most part out of the great cathedral schools, and theology was the senior faculty. Theology, moreover, was, notwithstanding the grip upon it of the forms and structure of Aristotelian logic, again and again the exciting subject, which evoked enthusiasm, and

---

[1] Cited from the article by G. F. A. Best, *Journal of Theological Studies* n.s. XIV (1963), p. 363.

correspondingly *odium*. One needs to name only Abelard, at the beginning of the medieval development, and Luther, at the end of it, to give some indication of the explosive quality of thinking and teaching that the theological faculties could generate. Nor has this quality of theological work ceased since the sixteenth century. There is no need to enter into rivalry with our colleagues in Classics and Oriental Studies; we can without fear of contradiction claim that many of the discoveries of modern archaeological and philological method, and the application to ancient texts of the historico-critical method, have been made, prompted, encouraged, or adapted and developed within the context of theological studies.

Again, theology for the minister is no more vocational than classics for the classics master; and, though one remembers the famous cable sent from Calcutta to Oxford—"Send tramway manager, classic preferred"—the teaching of classics is a likely fate for many of those who read classics in a university. I would venture the opinion that, in this sense, theology is less vocational than classics, highly as I respect the educational value of a classics course. The preacher must employ theological material and theological method, but he does so in constantly varying circumstances. If the truths he deals in do not change, they have to be applied in contexts of thought, social structure, and personal life that change from year to year, almost from day to day. In comparison, there is an unvarying quality not only in the form but also in the application of the pluperfect subjunctive, and he is a rare schoolboy who sees in—shall we say, the story of the Gracchi?—something that challenges him to reflect deeply upon, and to take action in, his own political environment.

So far I have been giving a rather superficial answer to the prima facie case that accuses theology of intruding where it does not belong, among the sciences. If we are to go further, we must tackle the question: What is theology? What is the study of theology? If we can analyse these questions, we may hope to understand both what the study of theology means to theologians, and what our study of theology may mean to our colleagues who are not theologians.

I begin on the lowest level and work up. It may be said first that theology as practised in good schools of theology affords an admirable educational discipline. There is a breadth, depth, and exactness of scholarship in theology which can be paralleled but are not easily surpassed.

The study of theology requires a linguistic discipline which in rigour equals that of any other school, and in breadth surpasses nearly all. Latin we expect. We demand an exact knowledge of Greek—Hellenistic Greek, it is true, but we know now that this is not simply "bad" Greek. No man escapes from a school of theology without knowing something of careful syntactical and semantic analysis; this is the main tool of the New Testament exegete. To Latin and Greek we add another language from a completely different linguistic family—Hebrew; and this is not merely an addition. It requires the student to adjust his mind to a completely different shape, for not only is the vocabulary of Hebrew quite fresh to the best of Grecians, the whole syntactical structure of the language is different. The student is required not only to know these languages but to study their interaction, as the Hebrew Old Testament gives place through the Septuagint to the Greek New. This is a severe enough discipline, and it is not everyone who can compass it; but the man who can and does has no need to feel small beer in comparison with colleagues in other departments. Anyone who, like Gibbon, can sneer at small but significant verbal distinctions—"I cannot forbear reminding the reader that the difference between the *Homoousion* and *Homoiousion* is almost invisible to the nicest theological eye"—shows himself to be in need of the discipline a good theological education would give him. In saying this I am far from defending the morals of the fourth-century Fathers, who employed far too many "blows and knocks" in proving their "doctrine orthodox". But if I were unable to see the difference between two significant words, even though they differ by only one letter, I should at least keep quiet about it.

The study of theology requires, secondly, all the methods and discipline of historical research. In biblical study alone, a theologian is required to achieve a fair measure of familiarity with some 1,500 years of crowded history; and for the greater part of this he is concerned not with religious history only but with the total history, so far as it is known, of a nation, whose contacts spread all over the Near East. The results of archaeology must be known and drawn upon, and the literature scientifically investigated. When historical study takes its turn, all the problems of the

Greek and Roman historian reappear, and ancient sagas, court records, scraps of biography and autobiography, poetic comment, and religious interpretation must be elucidated and evaluated. I speak here of the Old Testament; in the New the materials available for dealing with the historical problems are somewhat different, but the historical problem itself is just as important and just as acute.

The student of the Bible has, however, dealt only with the prolegomena of his real work when he has reconstructed the history to which his sources bear witness. As the Bible is not interested in history simply for its own sake, so neither is he. The biblical writers conceived history to be important as enshrining certain truths, or as at least forming the occasion for the uttering of certain truths. The theologian must go on to examine, collect, and weigh these truths, studying them first in the light of their original context, and then setting them in new contexts, making out of them a systematic whole. This is the beginning of theology as the term is commonly understood. Here, beyond the art of interpreting an ancient text, new techniques, skills, and information are called for. The history of doctrine must be known, not because the Church has always been right, but because it has sometimes been not far wrong, and because its mistakes are instructive; and the mind of the philosopher, capable of generalization, of inductive reason, and of system, is called for. In the end it becomes the task of theology to explain not religious experience only, but all experience.

I have run swiftly through this sketch of theological learning, concentrating mainly on those departments with which I myself have some familiarity, not with a view to suggesting that theologians are the Crichtons of scholarship but simply in order to show the vast range of properly academic discipline that theology includes. There is plenty here to open a man's eyes to the width of knowledge, and to train his ability in the most intricate, thorough, and exacting tasks and methods of pure scholarship.

We are ready now to take another step. Theology includes the study of the Christian tradition which runs like a thread through nineteen centuries of European history, and thus through all Western civilization. Anyone who wishes to understand this civilization, whether or not he himself is a Christian, cannot afford to neglect this thread. Sometimes in reaction and resistance, often in misunderstanding, the West has had to grapple with the Church and its teaching, and to come to terms with a Christian way of life. The future may well be different; no one can dispute the past. A further point, developing this, can be made. Christianity is a thread that runs through European history; religion is a thread that runs through the whole story of man. Again, it makes no difference to the immediate point whether one likes religion or dislikes it; the most unreligious of men will not deny that religion is an almost universal element in the make-up of humanity. As such, it is a proper subject of academic study. Moreover, though Christianity is not simply to be identified with religion, it has commonly been presented to mankind in the form of religion; indeed, notwithstanding the modern fashion, it may very well be questioned whether Christianity can ever be entirely divorced from religion and presented in a religionless form. It is not to be identified with religion, but it is perhaps anti-religious rather than religionless. Be that as it may: for most people, Christianity is expressed in religious, and occasionally also in cultic forms; and this means that the study of religion becomes relevant at the same time for the anthropologist and for the Christian theologian; and the latter must undoubtedly play a large part in the exploration and explanation of the exaltation, the baseness, and the sheer oddness of the human race.

So far so good. It may be granted that theologians behave in a reputable way, and that what they do is worth doing. They are engaged upon the task of interpreting a significant body of ancient literature, and it is a task few would disparage. True, some may prefer Plato to Isaiah, Seneca to St Paul (and for sheer entertainment, Aristophanes to all the lot); but the books of the Bible have stood the test of time, the test of sheer survival, and the odds are that anything that has held men's attention for a couple of millennia is worth attending to, for one reason or another. The theologian is also concerned with the religious element in man and society, and this, for good or ill, is no insignificant element. He handles the tradition which (again, for good or ill) runs through the story of Western thought, economics, and politics. Here he himself has a worth-while task to perform, with the opportunity of making "a contribution to knowledge", and of doing service to his colleagues. Even now, however, we are still scratching the surface and making little penetration. We have not answered the charge that the theologian is *ex hypothesi* prejudiced. Is it true to say of the theologian that for him "there are no ultimate authorities, no orthodoxies to which the pupil must subscribe"?

It all depends (if one may use the cliché) on what you mean by theology. For my part, I think there is a place for the handing out of doctrinal orthodoxy. Not all our forefathers were fools, and you cannot yourself work out every detail from the ground upwards. Moreover, the Church, both our own Church in particular and the totality of Churches in general, knows what it believes, and has a right to expect that those who represent it in public will represent it faithfully. This is legitimate enough, and as obvious as that one would not be suffered to use a Conservative platform to expound and advocate socialism. But this is not yet the critical theology that is the proper sphere of academic work. Perhaps it is easier to say what critical theology is not than to define what it is. For a positive statement one is driven almost at once at least to begin with the field of one's own specialism. I begin, therefore, with biblical study and biblical criticism.

Any man who in these days claimed to handle any field of history without prejudice or presupposition would certainly be laughed at; no one will claim that he begins his biblical study without presuppositions. This matters little. What does matter is the recognition that the presuppositions exist, and the constant conscious effort to reduce them as far as possible, and beyond that limit to allow for them. There is no proper biblical criticism that does not exercise this freedom; biblical study that has an end in view, that seeks to support a particular orthodox thesis, is not worthy of the name. Indeed, it has been said, and I think truly, that the only true criticism is sceptical criticism. At the time Bishop van Mildert was stoutly maintaining orthodoxy in Durham, a resident in the Theologische Stift in Tübingen was striking out the lines of radical biblical scholarship. I quote from an article of F. C. Baur's, written in 1836:

> One could very much wish that those people who so stoutly resist critical investigation would not give themselves the appearance of directing their opposition only against sceptical criticism, and not against criticism in general. If they were to take their language seriously they would have to agree that such

a distinction cannot, partly in itself and partly in particular from their own standpoint, be made. A criticism that is not allowed to be also a sceptical criticism is no criticism at all, because so often only doubt can lead to truth, and a theology that maintains the fundamental proposition that one ought never to doubt or to examine, would do best to strike historical criticism out of the list of theological disciplines.[1]

I have related my theme first of all to my own field of biblical criticism and historical research; but it has wider applications. The dogmatic theologian is not merely free to listen to the sounds and voices of which the air he breathes is full; he is under obligation to listen to them, and to make use of them, precisely as the writers of Scripture themselves did. There is no theological tradition he may not, and should not question. The same scepticism that the biblical critic brings to his given material, the philosophical theologian will bring to his.

It may be said: You go too far. By accommodating yourself to the critical, sceptical attitude of the world of learning you have cut the nerve of faith and pulled away the foundation of the Church, of which you profess yourself to be a servant. But this is not so. If it were, I should certainly not have chosen to speak on these lines on such occasion as this. I quote again from Baur:

Each of the two nourishes and refreshes itself from the other, and just as learning can only gain from faith, so faith can only gain from learning. Only from faith does learning discover how to purge itself from everything strange and foreign and give itself undividedly and unconditionally to its holy object, the truth, and again faith owes it to learning that it does not degenerate into stagnant quiescence but is kept in fresh and living movement, so as constantly to become more clearly and immediately conscious of its divine content. . . . For what matters is not how much a man believes, but only what he believes and how he believes, whether he believes in such a way as to know how to distinguish the true from the false, the

---

[1] *Abgenöthigte Erklärung gegen einen Artikel der evangelischen Kirchenzeitung, herausgegeben von D. E. W. Hengstenberg, Prof. der Theol. an der Universität zu Berlin. Mai 1836*, reprinted in *Ausgewählte Werke in Einzelausgaben*, herausgegeben von Klaus Scholder, 1 (Stuttgart 1963), p. 307.

certain from the uncertain, and the essential from the less essential.[1]

If the Church were simply identifiable with an institution, and truth with a credal formula, then indeed theology would cease to be an academic discipline, however learned theologians might be. So far as theologians do make these identifications, they exclude themselves from equal intellectual commerce with their colleagues in other disciplines. But no theologian is required by his subject-matter, by his own terms of reference, to do this. The Bible itself knows no handy, external method for distinguishing false prophets from true, and reminds its readers that we walk by faith, not by sight. It is this fact that compels the intelligent Christian, and in particular the professional theologian, to constant sifting, examination, revaluation. If he is too lazy, or too cowardly, to face this process, he not only abdicates his academic responsibility, he apostasizes from the faith. Apostasy is far more likely to come from failure to think than from excess of critical zeal. Theology, one might say, never is, but is always becoming.

I should, I think, be prepared on these grounds to defend theology as not merely *scientia* but *regina scientiarum*, because it is thus compelled by an inward necessity to be, in the strictest and most significant sense of the word, critical. I illustrate this once more, in a particular field, by another quotation:

> The critical and historical study of the New Testament is therefore the prime activity of the Church . . . It is commonly supposed that the modern method of historical investigation has been perfected outside the field of Biblical studies, and that it has been applied to the Bible. The opposite is, however, nearer to the truth. The method emerged from the heart of Biblical study, and was perfected by Christian theologians in order to enable them to handle literary and historical problems presented by the Scriptures. The method thus evolved has exerted a creative influence upon the general study of history. Nor is this fortuitous. Christian theology has been creative in the field of historical investigation, because the theologian has been compelled to a delicate sense for the importance of history by a faith which is grounded upon a particular event.[2]

[1] Op. cit., p. 301.
[2] E. Hoskyns and N. Davey, *The Riddle of the New Testament* (1931), pp. 10f.

The great importance of this quotation is that it suggests the fact that the freedom and confidence of investigation which a true theology engenders, and perhaps some of its methods too, may be handed on by theology to other fields. Here is the greatest service that theologians can render to their colleagues. Theology has learnt the lesson that men live by faith, not by sight, and at the same time has a sure confidence that the man who questions everything he can see will, nevertheless, find that his faith is not disappointed; having learnt this where it matters most, it will proceed to encourage a like freedom in other fields. The man who, in the freedom of faith, knows that he is not saved by belonging to the Church as an institution, or by assenting to the language of the Athanasian Creed, will be under no illusions about the soteriological efficacy of the Royal Society or the laws of thermodynamics, of the Arts Council or the principles of logical positivism. The theology of faith becomes the charter of humane studies and of science.

This is no light-hearted undertaking. We began by putting a question-mark beside theology; we finish by putting a question-mark beside every discipline in the world of learning. The truth of this has been so well put by Barth that I cannot do better than quote him as I draw to a close.

The theme of theology is grace, the absolute "Moment", the greedy dialectic of time and eternity. Other sciences have attempted, more or less successfully, to arrange an understanding with it in order that they may remain secure; but theology menaces them all . . . Theology owes its existence in history and its place in the *universitas litterarum* only to this essential, final, necessary, venture, and to its abnormal, irregular, revolutionary attack. Only by means of this venture and of this attack can it retain its status. It cannot retain its status if its primary purpose be the service of the Church. Still less can it live on what it has borrowed from the laboratory of historical research! . . . And so, as the Church sets a question-mark and a mark of exclamation at the outermost edge of civilization, so theology performs the same necessary role at the outermost edge of a university . . . Happy the man who is not required to stand in this precarious position; but woe to those who stand there, and know not what they do![1]

[1] K. Barth, *The Epistle to the Romans*, tr. E. C. Hoskyns (Oxford 1933), pp. 530f.

Or, to put it the other way round: it is not by abrogating its position as an exact science but by fulfilling it that theology serves the Church; and its service to the Church is that it queries its existence, and points men to the life that is lived by faith only.

SELECT INDEX

1. New Testament passages discussed

2. Modern Authors

3. Names and Subjects